Software Testing in the Real World

ACM PRESS BOOKS

This book is published as part of ACM Press Books – a collaboration between the Association for Computing Machinery and Addison-Wesley Publishing Company. ACM is the oldest and largest educational and scientific society in the information technology field. Through its high-quality publications and services, ACM is a major force in advancing the skills and knowledge of IT professionals throughout the world. For further information about ACM contact:

ACM Member Services
1515 Broadway, 17th Floor
New York, NY 10036-5701
Phone: +1-212-626-0500
Fax: +1-212-944-1318
E-mail: ACMHELP@ACM.org

ACM European Service Center
Avenue Marcel Thiry 204
1200 Brussels, Belgium
Phone: +32-2-774-9602
Fax: +32-2-774-9690
E-mail: ACM_Europe@ACM.org

OTHER TITLES IN THE SERIES

Software Testing
in the Real World

Improving the Process

Edward Kit

Edited by
Susannah Finzi

ADDISON-WESLEY

Harlow, England • Reading, Massachusetts • Menlo Park, California
New York • Don Mills, Ontario • Amsterdam • Bonn • Sydney • Singapore
Tokyo • Madrid • San Juan • Milan • Mexico City • Seoul • Taipei

Cover designed by Op den Brouw, Design & Illustration, Reading and printed by The Riverside Printing Co. (Reading) Ltd.
Typeset by Wyvern Typesetting Ltd.
Text designed by Sally Grover.

Printed in the United States of America

First printed in 1995. Reprinted in 1996.

ISBN 0-201-87756-2

British Library Cataloguing in Publication Data
A catalogue record for this book is available from the British Library.

Library of Congress Cataloging in Publication Data
Kit, Edward.
    Software testing in the real world : improving the process /
Edward Kit ; edited by Susannah Finzi.
        p.   cm. — (ACM Press books)
    Includes bibliographical references and index.
    ISBN 0-201-87756-2
    1. Computer software—Testing.   I. Finzi, Susannah.   II. Title.
III. Series.
QA76. 76. T48K58   1995
005. 1'4—dc20   95-37212
                                                                      CIP

Foreword

Over the years I have had the occasion to meet and work with many wonderful and talented people in the testing field. Ed Kit holds a special place among that group. He has personally contributed to the development of better testing practices from many perspectives – as a software practitioner, a testing and quality manager, and as a seminar leader and consultant. I have personally learned a lot from Ed and found it a real pleasure to know and work with him professionally for almost a decade. This book is one more way in which Ed is contributing to our field and helping all of us share in his special insights.

The book was derived as an outgrowth of Ed's experiences with "real-world" testing concerns and issues. It has a strong emphasis and focus on the testing process and how to improve it. From the practical, down to earth idea of keeping a running list of potential improvements as you read the book (The clean-sheet approach to getting started in Chapter 3), to the many tips and exercises sprinkled throughout, to the eight appendices that include overviews of the standards relevant to testing as well as references and pointers to testing resources and tools; the book is chock full of practical ideas that most readers should find easy to understand and apply.

Part II is particularly on target for the novice or individual working in an immature organization. The chapters establish what testing is (or should be) all about and provide a framework for ongoing process improvement. Even though much of what is described may properly be viewed as "common sense", the real-world reality is that getting it effectively practiced remains distinctly "uncommon"! *Software Testing in the Real World* should go a long way toward helping many of us to make practical and lasting improvements.

The book is easy to read and suitable for anyone interested in how to achieve better testing.

Most readers, especially practicing developers, testers, and managers, should be well pleased. I encourage you to "test" it out. Many of you may have read my now nearly decade-old book, *The Complete Guide to Software Testing*. This book offers a fresh updated perspective and covers many of the topics and issues that I wish I had found time to update and write about myself. I'd love to know what you particularly like and find you can put to use for real-world benefit. Please feel free to write and share your test results!

Bill Hetzel
President, Software Quality Engineering

Preface

Software testing.
It is exhilarating. It is exasperating.
It can be the best of jobs – or the worst.
It is fundamental to delivering quality software on time within budget.

This book is for anyone interested in improving their test process, including test specialists, product developers, managers, quality assurance specialists, maintainers, project managers, auditors, systems analysts, tool developers, and others whose jobs involve understanding software testing. It offers developers and other people whose work is not primarily in the testing area an opportunity to improve their own specialty through a better understanding of testing.

To understand testing and to improve testing practice, it is essential to see the software testing process in its broadest terms – as the means by which people, methodology, tools, measurement, and leadership are integrated to test a software product. More than 20 years in testing practice, teaching, and consulting have shown me the following key questions raised again and again by people wanting to improve their testing process:

Methodology questions

- What are the key testing methods, when do we use them, and how do we implement them?
- How do we prevent defect migration and improve defect finding capabilities?
- How can we understand and leverage the relevant test standards and terminology?
- How do we create meaningful test plans and other critical test deliverables?
- How do we identify and prioritize potential software testing process improvements?

Leadership questions

- How do we organize the software testing effort so it is measurable and controllable?
- Where can we find additional help regarding software testing?
- How can we ensure that improvements are sustainable in the medium and long term?

- How can we organize testing for the most effective relations between people?
- How can we generally maximize exhilaration and minimize exasperation?

Tools and technology questions

- What are the most significant opportunities for automating the testing process?
- How can we use measurement to understand and control the software test process?
- How can we select test tools and vendors and implement an effective tools program?
- How can we use risk analysis techniques as a basis for decision making in testing?

My experience has shown that a balanced strategy addressing methodology, leadership, and technology is most effective for improving testing.

Most software development organizations suffer from immature software processes. Given this starting point, practitioners and managers naturally ask: "Yes, but what do I do now?". This book offers a tool-box for effectively improving the software testing process. A tool-box is not a single methodology to be followed from A to Z. It is a menu of techniques that can be taken individually or in combination to provide the means to formulate and reach realistic improvement objectives.

Part I is for orientation. It describes the six essentials of software testing, the history of testing, and a simple, practical approach to getting started with improving the testing process. It identifies software engineering in general and testing in particular as new disciplines grappling with the escalating demands of an environment expecting miracles.

Part II establishes practical goals from a "now we are here" position, and explains how these relate to formal and less formal definitions of testing and testing objectives, and to the current standards that are fundamental (and useful) to practitioners in their everyday work.

The basic forms of the testing process are explained, and the critical real-world issues of cost and risk are fully clarified and integrated in the decision making process of what, when and how to test. In this part we address the items that need to be in place before we dig more deeply into the testing activities of verification and validation. The issues of planning, software engineering maturity goals, configuration management, standards, and tools are explained and positioned.

Part III explains the basic verification and validation testing tasks, including planning and controlling testing costs, and making the best use of resources. The use of tools as a way of gaining leverage in the various testing activities is explained, together with clarification of tool categories, and practical guidance on the critical questions for tool acquisition. The appropriate and constructive use of measurement is explained, and guidelines given for the proper use of measurement results.

Part IV explains the organizational and human management issues that surround the test effort and which are key determinants of its success. It surveys some current best practice sources, and then refocuses on how to get sustainable improvements in place in the short and medium term.

Definitions, references, and examples are integrated within the main text of the book as far as possible. The appendices contain a variety of material that is too detailed for inclusion in the main text of the book, and which is essentially complementary. This includes sample checklists, exercises, planning documents, and sample working documents. There is further detail on official standards and specifications as well as useful help sources such as journals, tools, conferences, newsletters, user groups, and an annotated bibliography.

Acknowledgments

Life provides many teachers. Some say all of life is our teacher. Space prohibits acknowledging all who have positively influenced this book, but does allow acknowledgment of the following people due special appreciation.

Great appreciation is due my wife, Cathy Baldwin, who not only provided continuous moral support and endless editing of the book, but also provided encouragement during the early start-up years of Software Development Technologies. Special thanks to our families for their support over the years.

I am particularly grateful to David Gelperin and Bill Hetzel: to David for providing the opportunity to teach my first course on software testing nearly a decade ago, and for providing the ongoing friendship and support that kept me going; to Bill for encouraging me to write a book and for writing the foreword for the book; and to both of them for providing the opportunity to be associated with Software Quality Engineering for many years.

Appreciation is due Chris Larson, who for 15 years has generously shared his friendship and wealth of software engineering experiences gained from over 25 years with Hewlett Packard, IBM, Tandem, and CDC, and who contributed enormously to the course on which this book is based.

Appreciation is also due Susannah Finzi for being an outstanding friend and editor, and for keeping the book appealing from a global perspective while patiently enduring seemingly endless rewrites without a single complaint.

Appreciation is due the reviewers who gave their time to provide valuable comments, especially Bill Hetzel, David Gelperin, Dot Graham, Marty Gipson, Vijay Sarathy, Ray O'Neal, Ellen Brodbine, Trevor Reeve, Cathy Baldwin, Chris Larson, Denise Leigh, and Paul Claydon.

Finally, appreciation is due to the students who attended the courses upon which this book is based and who in the process became my teachers and provided suggestions for improving the course, especially the participants from Hewlett Packard, Motorola, Microsoft, Apple Computer, US Army, IBM, NCR, Johnson & Johnson, Grumman Data Systems, Australia and New Zealand Bank, ADP, EDS, PeopleSoft, SCO, General Electric, Oracle, NEC, Lloyds Bank, USDA, NetFrame, Cadence, Sears, AT&T, Informix, British Aerospace, Sybase, Tandem, and Octel Communications.

Ed Kit
Cupertino, September 1995

Contents

PART I

Software testing process maturity

"The journey towards excellence is a never ending road"

H. JAMES HARRINGTON, The Improvement Process

Chapter 1
The six essentials of software testing

This chapter describes the fundamentals for engineering a new software testing process or renovating one currently in existence. The software testing process is the means by which people, methods, measurements, tools, and equipment are integrated to test a software product. The essentials of the software testing process that serve as the foundation for this book are:

(1) The quality of the test process determines the success of the test effort.
(2) Prevent defect migration by using early life-cycle testing techniques.
(3) The time for software testing tools is now.
(4) A real person must take responsibility for improving the testing process.
(5) Testing is a professional discipline requiring trained, skilled people.
(6) Cultivate a positive team attitude of creative destruction.

Essential 1: The quality of the test process determines the success of the test effort

The quality of a software system is primarily determined by the quality of the software process that produced it. Likewise, the quality and effectiveness of software testing are primarily determined by the quality of the test processes used.

Testing has its own cycle. The testing process begins with the product requirements phase and from there parallels the entire development process. In other words, for each phase of the development process there is an important testing activity.

Test groups that operate within organizations having an immature development process will feel more pain than those that don't. But regardless of the state of maturity of the development organization, the test group can and should focus on improving its own internal process. An immature test process within an immature development organization will result in an unproductive, chaotic, frustrating environment that produces low-quality results and unsatisfactory products. People effectively renovating a testing process within that same immature organization will serve as a catalyst for improving the development process as a whole.

Essential 2: Prevent defect migration by using early life-cycle testing techniques

More than half the errors are usually introduced in the requirements phase. The cost of errors is minimized if they are detected in the same phase as they are introduced, and an effective test program prevents the migration of errors from any development phase to any subsequent phases.

While many of us are aware of this, in practice we often do not have mechanisms in place to detect these errors until much later – often not until function and system test, at which point we have entered "The Chaos Zone". Chances are that we are currently missing the best opportunity for improving the effectiveness of our testing if we are not taking advantage of the proven testing techniques that can be applied early in the development process.

For example, we should learn to perform reviews on critical documents like requirements. Even an immature organization can implement an effective inspections program. Inspections have proven a winner repeatedly for well over 20 years, and have been justified (and documented) in cost/benefit terms over and over again.

Essential 3: The time for software testing tools is now

After many years of observation, evaluation, and mostly waiting, we can now say the time for testing tools has arrived. There is a wide variety of tool vendors to choose from, many of which have mature, healthy products.

For example, test-cycle time reductions and automation providing for 24 hours a day of unattended test operations can be achieved with capture/playback tools. There is one for every major platform: some are more intrusive than others; some are appropriate for client/server; some are technically elaborate to use; others are simple.

Another type of essential tool is the structural coverage tool. Used to determine if the software has been thoroughly tested, this tool tells us specifically which parts of the product have in fact been executed by our tests. It is no longer acceptable to expect our customers to be the first to execute our code!

It is important to have a strategy for tool acquisition, and a proper procedure for handling tool selection. While such procedures are based on common sense, they do need to be systematically implemented. Tool acquisition is an area where there may be a strong case for seeking independent expert advice.

Essential 4: A real person must take responsibility for improving the testing process

If the testing group is feeling pain, start campaigning for improvements to a few of the key issues, such as better specifications, and better reviews and inspections.

Management should appoint an architect or small core team to prioritize potential improvements and lead the testing improvement effort, and must make it clear that they will give their ongoing support. It is not rocket science, but it takes effort – and time. Tools can help tremendously, but they must be used within an overall test process that includes effective test planning and design.

When all is said and done, software testing is a process that requires people who take responsibility for its improvement. For the testing process to improve, someone must plan and manage the progress.

Essential 5: Testing is a professional discipline requiring trained, skilled people

Software testing has become a profession – a career choice – and a place to make our mark. The software testing process has evolved considerably, and has reached the point where it is a discipline requiring trained professionals. To succeed today, an organization must be adequately staffed with skilled software testing professionals who get proper support from management.

Testing is not an entry level job or stepping stone to other things. Many people find that when done properly, it surpasses the challenge of product development. It should be organized so it can faithfully maintain allegiance to the customer. It should not be subservient to or be positioned for easy overrule by the product development or any other organization.

Testing should be independent, unbiased, and organized for the fair sharing of recognition and rewards for contributions made to product quality.

Essential 6: Cultivate a positive team attitude of creative destruction

Testing requires disciplined creativity. Good testing, that is devising and executing successful tests – tests that discover the defects in a product – requires real ingenuity, and may be viewed as destructive. Indeed, considerable creativity is needed to destroy something in a controlled and systematic way. Good testers are methodically taking the product apart, finding its weaknesses, pushing it up to, and beyond, its limits.

Can we make this product fail to do what we expect it to do? When is it going to break? We know it's going to break, because we can always find errors. But is it breaking at reasonable boundaries? Is it stressing or breaking acceptably or unacceptably, given its criticality? Do we know that we have covered all the important possibilities? It is the testers who supply this information, and it is only when we're satisfied that these questions, and many others, have been properly addressed, that we should ship the product to our customer.

Establishing the proper "test to break" mental attitude has a profound effect on testing success. If the objective is to show that the product does what it shouldn't do, and doesn't do what it should, we're on the way to testing success. Although far from the norm today, the results that we get when practitioners and their managers together cultivate this attitude of disciplined, creative destruction are nothing less than astonishing.

Successful testing requires a methodical approach. It requires us to focus on the basic critical factors: planning, project and process control, risk management, inspections, measurement, tools, organization – and professionalism. Remember that testers make a vital positive contribution throughout the development process to ensure the quality of the product.

Chapter 2

The state of the art and the state of the practice

For centuries our effort to understand and control our environment by complex disciplines has evolved largely through painful trial and disastrous error. Eventually, basic know-how, guidelines and best practices evolve, and become second nature to practicing professionals in their particular fields.

In the evolutionary scale of human disciplines, software engineering still flounders in the primeval mud. When it feels like this in our own organization, it's worth remembering how young the software development discipline really is. Even the phrase "software engineering," implying a systematic approach with ground rules, was not used until the late 1960s.

Furthermore, the gap between the state of the art and the state of the practice is a chasm that, if anything, becomes wider. Software testing, for instance, has yet to become a fundamental component of university software engineering curricula, and training in industry is improving but often haphazard. Papers are published (though not always read by those who need them most) presenting leading-edge ways of doing software better and achieving desirable levels of software quality in particular, but many of these state-of-the-art methods are unproven in the field, and many omit real-world dimensions like return on investment.

Even the many well-proven methods are largely unused in industry today, and the development of software systems remains inordinately expensive, fraught with costly errors, and often late, with products often costing far more to maintain over their lifetime than to develop in the first place.

At the same time, the systems we build are ever more complex and critical, and more than 50% of the development effort is frequently spent on testing. Yet many of the people responsible for this testing are still struggling for a viable working platform, properly equipped with useful, available test tools and an independent, properly organized and resourced position in the software development environment.

The short eventful history of a very new discipline

The notion of software engineering implies, among other things, an attempt to achieve reliability, functionality, predictability, economy, and efficiency. Software testing concerns itself with all of these.

In the early days of software development, this concern was rather narrowly interpreted. Testing was regarded as "debugging", or fixing the known bugs in the software, and was usually performed by the developers themselves. There were rarely any dedicated resources for testing, and those that were dedicated got involved very late in the development process, often only after the product was coded and nearly complete. In the worst examples, this is still the case.

By 1957 software testing was distinguished from debugging and became regarded as detecting the bugs in the software. But testing was still an after-development activity, with the attitude of "let's push it around a little bit just to show ourselves that the product actually works." The underlying objective was to convince ourselves that it worked – and then ship it. The universities did not talk much about testing either. Computer science curricula dealt with numerical methods and algorithm development, but not with software engineering or testing. First compilers, then operating systems and then data bases were the prime focus, but none of these were helpful in getting people to address testing issues in the real world of industry.

By the 1970s "software engineering" as a term was used more often, though there was little consensus as to what it really meant. The first formal conference on testing was held at the University of North Carolina in 1972, and a series of publications followed (Hetzel, 1973; Myers 1976, 1979).

It was Myers (1979) who saw that the self-fulfilling nature of human goals had a major impact on testing work. He defined testing as "the process of executing a program with the intent of finding errors." He pointed out that if our goal is to show the absence of errors, we will discover very few of them. If our goal is to show the presence of errors, we will discover a large number of them. Establishing the proper goal and mind-set has a profound effect on testing success (see Chapter 4).

The work of Myers and others in the 1970s was a major step in the development of satisfactory testing processes, but in the real world of industry, testing continued to be at the top of the list of things that got dumped when the schedules and the budget became tight. Testing was started too late in the process, and there was not enough time to do it properly when it did start. Management would even short-circuit it altogether with, "well let's just ship the product anyway because we don't have time to test it" (i.e., because the rewards appear to outweigh the risks). If this sounds at all familiar, it is because in many organizations this is still common practice.

By the early 1980s "Quality!" became the battle cry. Software developers and testers started to get together to talk about software engineering and testing. Groups were formed that eventually created many of the standards we have today. These standards, like the IEEE (Institute of Electrical and Electronics Engineers) and ANSI (American National Standards Institute) standards in the USA or the ISO (International Standards Organization) international standards, are now becoming too weighty to digest in their full published form for everyday practical purposes. However, they do include important guidelines, a good baseline for contracts, and provide an invaluable reference.

In the 1990s testing tools finally came into their own. It is now widely understood that tools are not only merely useful, but absolutely vital to adequate testing of the systems built today, and we are seeing the development of a wide variety of tools to help with the testing process. By now almost every company developing software has somebody looking into tools, and tools have become a critical part of the testing process. However, on their own, like most techniques, they don't solve the real problem.

Development and testing evolution

	1960	1970	1995
Software size	small	moderate	very large
Degree of software complexity	low	medium	high
Size of development teams	small	medium	large
Development methods and standards	*ad hoc*	moderate	sophisticated
Test methods and standards	*ad hoc*	primitive	emerging
Independent test organizations	few	some	many
Recognition of testing's importance	little	some	significant
Number of testing professionals	few	few	many

Despite the enormous advances in the last 30 years, the software process (including the testing process) in most companies is still very immature. Furthermore, the complexity and criticality of the problems which software is expected to solve have become greater, and platform complexities have become bigger, and this is tending to out-run our ability to put more effective methods, tools, and professionals in place. It is no wonder that life gets increasingly tough for testers.

Where exactly are we now?

A proper understanding of the concept of the maturity of our software engineering practices is fundamental to our testing success. It is essential to know our present baseline and we need an objective assessment of the maturity level of the development environment in which we are operating and its impact on our test process.

During the 1980s, the Software Engineering Institute (SEI) at Carnegie Mellon University developed a software process assessment method and capability maturity model for the United States Department of Defense. Their 1987 technical report proposed a five-level capability maturity model. This is a practical model for organizations to measure their own level of software maturity.

The reality is that most organizations still have fairly immature software process development environments. About 75% of the world of software development is at level 1 on a scale of 1–5 in terms of really having mature software processes in place. When we talk about software testing in the real world, this 1 on the scale of 1–5 represents the actual environment in which we work and within which we have to do our testing.

The good news is that the SEI model also explains how to get from each level to the next. There are companies that have achieved level 5 status but they are in a very small minority (see Chapter 6 for more detail on the SEI and software engineering maturity, and Chapter 14 for current trends and best practice literature).

How should testing be positioned?

When testing was something that was done after development, a back-end activity after the code was finished, the development life cycle consisted of requirements, design, implementation and then test. We waited until the code was done and then we did some function testing. Errors were easy to find, and, not surprisingly, developers and testers often came to be seen as adversarial.

Once it was understood that testing was much more than debugging, it was also clear that testing was more than just a phase near the end of the development cycle. In fact early testing is a key to the success of the test effort. Testing has a life cycle of its own, and there is useful and constructive testing to be done throughout the entire life cycle of development (see Chapter 5).

We are talking about testing as the vehicle for detecting errors in the software, but we will use the term software to mean much more than just the code. The definition of software should include the related documentation such as the specifications, the design documents, and the user manuals.

The notion of engineering software quality means not just reliability and efficiency in the abstract, but something more closely linked to customer requirements and customer satisfaction. Furthermore, how does testing as carried out in most organizations today relate to quality assurance and the quality assurance (QA) function?

QA is not the same as process development. The QA function does not generally include moving the process ball forward, i.e., being a process expert and suggesting ways of implementing process improvements. QA is usually defined in the literature as a function which:

- monitors the software and the development processes that produce it;
- ensures full compliance with established standards and procedures for the software and the software process;
- ensures that inadequacies in the product, the process, or the standards are brought to management's attention.

In contrast to QA, testing performs in-depth analysis, testing, and overall evaluation of a software product or system. It is meant to represent the customer and as such primarily owes its allegiance to the customer rather than to development. This is widely understood, and yet in many organizations testing is still formally subordinate to development.

This subordination to development means the voice of testing often goes unheard. While the testing people do their job and report the results, they frequently find their management simply thanks them for their information, but ships the product anyway. Little or no real action is taken based on the testers' input, because testing often has no authority or power or control in the organization. This is frequently reflected in staffing policies, where it is sometimes assumed that testing is a place to put junior people or anyone who can be spared without their loss being felt elsewhere.

However, things are improving. The world understands, at least in theory, the importance of testing, the importance of having an independent testing function with a viable position in the organization, and the necessity to hire technically competent people and reward them adequately (see Chapter 13). Testing is coming to be seen as a profession with its own work products that are maintained as important assets of the organization (see Chapter 6).

References

Hetzel, W. (1973). *Program Test Methods*. Englewood Cliffs, NJ: Prentice-Hall.
Myers, G.J. (1976). *Software Reliability: Principles and Practices*. John Wiley.
Myers, G.J. (1979). *The Art of Software Testing*. John Wiley.

Chapter 3
The clean-sheet approach to getting started

In the following chapters the essentials of testing are developed in more detail as well as many techniques and ideas that are independently adaptable to any organization. Start now with a clean sheet of paper and keep a running list of potential improvements you believe are key to renovating the software testing process in your organization. These ideas for improvement may take many forms: a new idea you want to use; a new technique or tool you want to investigate; a fundamental change in the software test process. Consider objective, practical, cost-effective goals. Review and update this list from time to time as you read this book, and prioritize the entries. To get you started, a few suggestions are listed below. Others are given at the end of several of the chapters which follow.

Potential improvements

- Investigate what it would take to implement an effective inspections program.
- Launch an effort to determine what tools would provide the most leverage.
- Begin today to cultivate a "test to break" attitude of creative destruction.

At the end of the book, Appendix H gives a list of all the "Improvements to be implemented" created by a group of 11 testing professionals. These professionals came from widely different types of organizations with different levels of software engineering process maturity, and the list represents what they considered they could realistically attempt within their own organizations after attending the software testing course on which this book is based.

A second list in Appendix H was compiled during a testing course held on-site at a medium-sized software company. This time the list is organized under two headings: "Prioritized improvements internal to the software testing function" and "Prioritized improvements external to the software testing function." It is a good idea to identify the improvement ideas on your sheet as being internal or external to the testing group. It can also be useful to rate items to implement in terms of:

- the difficulty of implementing in the organization;
- the resources required for implementation;
- the payoff in improvement to the testing process;
- the short-, medium- or long-term effort required to (realistically) achieve the item.

This rating can be done as a second pass after the potential ideas have been assembled.

Remember to include long-term goals, too. Real progress is made in small steps over two, five, 10 years or more. We have discovered a few companies that do long-term plans, and are currently implementing their third 10-year plan!

Keep asking the right question: "Is what we are doing now an improvement over what we did before?" If the answer is yes, and yes again next time and the time after, then we are on the road to continuous improvement. It is surprising how much can be achieved with limited resources. Management and peer support will grow once improvements are visible to the organization.

PART II
The framework for test process improvement

"The will to win is important, but the will to prepare is crucial"

JOE PATERNO, Head Coach, Pennsylvania State University

Chapter 4
Establishing a practical perspective

Chapter 5
Critical choices: what, when, and how to test

Chapter 6
Critical disciplines: framework for testing

Chapter 4
Establishing a practical perspective

Software is written by people, and people make mistakes. In standard commercial software, errors are present. These errors are expensive; some more than others. We can't entirely prevent them being introduced, but we can work to locate them early, especially the most critical ones.

We need to understand and be able to implement appropriate testing techniques. But it is also important to consider some of the non-technical issues that help us toward a more successful testing effort, so we can not only test well, but also test smarter.

Definitions of the testing process and the elements within it are important. They are essential for communication and agreement with our collaborators on what we are doing, why, and how. They establish a common language, providing a foundation for future discussions. They help us get the right focus for our testing effort, so that we get beyond just putting out forest fires.

As testers, what we see as our mission, our basic professional attitude, can have a profound effect on the success of the testing effort and can provide a catalyst for improvement throughout the development process.

What are we aiming for?

What is the ultimate goal of testing? At the end of the line is the fact that we are in the business of making sure our customers are successful. It is our customers who pay the bills, and if we are to stay in business we have to solve their problems. Our underlying goal must be their delight and satisfaction. We aim for quality, but quality isn't just an abstract ideal. We are developing systems to be used, and used successfully, not to be admired on the shelf. If quality is to be a meaningful and useful goal in the real world, it must include the customer.

Testers are not in charge of the whole quality program. However, many testing decisions should ultimately be based on customer satisfaction. In large and complex development organizations, and in the hurly-burly of most software development projects, this is very easily forgotten. What do our customers want from the system? Will it deliver what they want when they use it? These are the practical questions that lie behind many testing decisions.

All you ever wanted to know about errors

Faults, failures, errors, defects, issues, bugs, mistakes. If these are the targets that testers spend their professional careers hunting down, it's important to know something about them.

The what and the why

Errors lurk in the work products of the software development process. Work products don't just mean code. They include product requirements, functional specifications, drafts and final versions of user manuals, drafts and final versions of data sheets, technical support notices and many other things which are all work products of different phases of the development process.

Software production can be seen as a series of imperfect translation processes. Each of these translations produces a work product or deliverable. Software errors are introduced when there is a failure to completely and accurately translate one representation to another, or to fully match the solution to the problem.

Software errors are human errors. Since all human activity, especially complex activity, involves error, testing accepts this fact and concentrates on detecting errors in the most productive and efficient ways it can devise.

There are several different terms used within this model of general failure to translate successfully (IEEE/ANSI, 1990 [Std 610.12-1990]):

- *Mistake*: A human action that produces an incorrect result.
- *Fault*: An incorrect step, process, or data definition in a computer program. The outgrowth of the mistake. (Potentially leads to a failure.)
- *Failure*: An incorrect result. The result (manifestation) of the fault (e.g., a crash).
- *Error*: The amount by which the result is incorrect.

Mistakes are what people make, and a mistake can be defined as the thing the person did wrong. The phone rang while we were coding, and while distracted we pressed the wrong key and the results of that mistake produced a fault or bug in our work product.

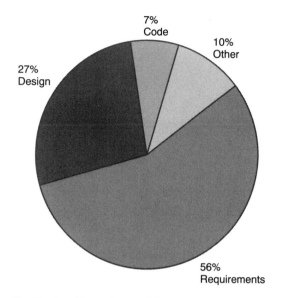

Figure 4.1 Defect distribution. Data obtained from a presentation entitled "Writing testable requirements", by Dick Bender (1993). The word "requirements" in this context includes the functional design. (© 1993, 1994 Software Development Technologies)

Failures are the manifestation of these faults. The fault or bug is there, within the documentation or the code, and even if it hasn't caused a failure yet, it's still a fault and it's the tester's job to find it.

When the failure manifests itself and the system goes down or the user gets the wrong message back or the cash-point provides the wrong amount of money, then according to the above definition, the amount by which that result is incorrect is the error.

Few people use these terms accurately, and in practice this is not very important. For the purposes of this book, defect or error is used most of the time. The important thing is to see that there are different types of things we are looking for when we are testing.

Where are errors?

A closer look at the common distribution of errors will help us to focus our test effort better and in the most productive place. There is strong evidence that errors are concentrated in the earlier stages of the development process, as shown in Figure 4.1.

Errors at the early stage are usually thick on the ground, and they also have the unpleasant habit of migration. Using the analogy of an assembly line in manufacturing, if a bad component or sub-assembly is allowed to enter the line, the unit to which it is attached is also "bad" from that point on. The problem increases as the unit progresses down the line and out of the door, and so does the cost of fixing it. In other words, errors are not self-contained. As they migrate to the units downstream, they take on new forms.

The cost of errors

All errors are costly. Undetected errors, as well as errors detected late in the development process, are the most expensive of all. Undetected errors will migrate downstream within the system to cause failures. If detected only at a later stage of development they entail costly rework. If not detected, they can cause failures in the field with serious financial and legal consequences, and (at best) high lifetime costs for the system.

This means that testing should be a continuous activity throughout the development cycle. It also means that testing the end product is only one battle – and certainly not the most cost-effective one to win – in the software quality war. Today, anything between 40% and 70% of initial software development time and resources can be devoted to error detection and removal. The bad news is that most organizations have not established a way of knowing what they actually do spend. However, any significant improvement in how testing resources are used can greatly reduce overall development costs. (For further development of the "test early" idea, see Chapter 5.)

So what *is* testing really? Some definitions

Definitions matter, although consensus as to what testing "really is" is less important than being able to use these definitions to focus our attention on the things that should happen when we are testing.

Historical definitions of testing

(1) Establishing confidence that a program does what it is supposed to do (Hetzel, 1973).
(2) The process of executing a program or system with the intent of finding errors (Myers, 1979).
(3) Detecting specification errors and deviations from the specification.
(4) Any activity aimed at evaluating an attribute or capability of a program or system (Hetzel, 1983).
(5) The measurement of software quality (Hetzel, 1983).
(6) The process of evaluating a program or system.
(7) Verifying that a system satisfies its specified requirements or identifying differences between expected and actual results.
(8) Confirming that a program performs its intended functions correctly.

All these definitions are useful, but in different ways. Some definitions (2) focus on what is done while testing (Myers, 1979); others focus on more general objectives like assessing quality (5) and customer satisfaction (1, 3), and others, like (7) and (8), focus on goals like expected results.

For example, if customer satisfaction is our goal (and it should be), this satisfaction, or what would constitute it, should be expressed in the requirements. In situations where requirements are well written and complete, we already have an important advantage. We can ask: "How good is our specification? Was it implemented properly?"

A definition (7) identifying differences between expected and actual results is valuable because it focuses on the fact that when we are testing we need to be able to anticipate what is supposed to happen. It is then possible to determine what actually does happen and compare the two. Without this comparison one of the fundamentals of testing is missing.

The IEEE/ANSI definitions of testing

(1) The process of operating a system or component under specified conditions, observing or recording the results, and making an evaluation of some aspect of the system or component (IEEE/ANSI, 1990 [Std 610.12-1990]).

(2) The process of analyzing a software item to detect the difference between existing and required conditions (that is, bugs) and to evaluate the features of the software items (IEEE/ANSI, 1983 [Std 829-1983]).

ANSI uses these two different definitions in the official standards, both of which are somewhat unsatisfactory and which appear to be validation-orientated. The first one, for instance, refers to "operating...under specified conditions", which implies that no testing can be done until there is something to operate.

For the purposes of this book, we want to make sure that our definitions of testing do not preclude the testing of documents like specifications. One kind of testing, verification, can be performed on any work product – any intermediate product in the development cycle. The other kind of testing, validation, can only be performed by executing the code (see Chapter 5).

Managers have their own views and definitions of testing, which reflect different priorities and different pressures from those of the testers. Managers want to know that the product is safe and reliable and that it will function properly under normal and adverse conditions. Managers also want to know that the product is what the users want, so they can ship it and start making some money.

Quality is also important to managers. They want to establish confidence in their products to get future business. For them financial issues will, quite properly, always play an important part in decisions, and they want to be sure they won't get sued.

Most importantly, what about testers themselves? What is a good working definition, that will focus testers' attention on the essentials of the testing job?

The best definition for the tester
The purpose of testing is to discover errors. Testing is the process of trying to discover every conceivable fault or weakness in a work product. (Myers, 1979)

Good testers have a testing attitude

What does testing mean to testers?

Testers hunt errors

If the testers' job is to find every conceivable fault or weakness in the work product, then a good test is one that has a good probability of detecting an as yet undiscovered error, and a successful test is one that detects an as yet undiscovered error.

The focus on showing the presence of errors is the basic attitude of a good tester. It is our job, and it is what gives us personal satisfaction. We feel good on the days when we find defects, and we're thrilled when we've exceeded our error-finding goal for the day or the week. Detected errors are celebrated – for the good of the product.

Testers are destructive – but creatively so

Testing is a positive and creative effort of destruction. It takes imagination, persistence and a strong sense of mission to systematically locate the weaknesses in a complex structure and to demonstrate its failures. This is one reason why it is particularly hard to test our own work. There is a natural real sense in which we don't want to find errors in our own material.

When we test our own material we start with the viewpoint that it works. It works the way we've constructed it. When trying to test our own material we know where the boundaries and the problems are, but we don't think they're big problems, or that anyone will have to confront them (or their consequences) at some later stage. As the developer of the material, our "mind set" is that it's good the way it is, so we test it, but not too hard. What we need is someone else who can attack it with the attitude of: "I'm here to destroy this thing. I'm going to find the defects that I know are there; that's my job and that's what I'm paid to do."

Testers pursue errors, not people

Errors are in the work product, not in the person who made the mistake. With the "test to destroy" attitude, we are not attacking an individual in the organization or a team of developers, but we are looking for errors in those developers' work products.

Developers need to understand that testers are not "against" them in finding errors in their products, but are there to help them because the developers themselves don't have the time, the skills or tools – or the objective viewpoint – to test their own products. It is important to get the relationship defined, and here testers can take the initiative: "You're specialists in development. That's what you do best. We're going to take the time to learn how to do testing; we're going to find out what tools are out there; we're going to become specialists in the testing area. Together we'll build better products."

The key is to manage the developers and testers as a team. The testers' role in the team is to find the defects and put them on the table, which can make developers defensive. A fine balance must be struck between being adversaries in the sense of finding errors in the developers' work products, and being part of a single team with them in producing the final product. It helps a great deal if the development and testing functions are well organized. Independence is important, but the "play team attitude" can often be fostered and assisted in simple practical ways.

Get meetings going to discuss problem areas with development and marketing people. Ensure problem discussions are focused on the problems in the product and not on the people who we think may have been responsible for producing them.

Testers add value

Everybody – testers, developers, marketing people, and managers – needs to understand that testers are adding value to the product by discovering errors and getting them on the table as early as possible; to save the developers from building products based on error-ridden sources, to ensure the marketing people can deliver what the customer wants, and to ensure management gets the bottom line on the quality and finance they are looking for.

There can be a great sense of accomplishment and positive team spirit in finding the defects, helping developers do their jobs better, and ultimately seeing that the company sends out sound products. The aim is to produce a high-quality product, and prevent the pain we will suffer if it isn't done successfully. One consequence, if we don't succeed, is that we're going to have unhappy customers who are going to sue us – and we'll all be out of jobs.

If management can actively promote awareness of the team attitude in both testers and developers, so much the better, but the initiative often has to be with the testers who are in a good position to understand their own particular contribution to quality (see Chapter 13).

How testers do it

Having gotten the "tester attitude," how do we go about detecting errors?

- by examining the internal structure and design?
- by examining the functional user interface?
- by examining the design objectives?
- by examining the users' requirements?
- by executing code?

The answer is that we have to do all these things, and many more.

In the real world, under schedule pressure from customers and others, senior management can set deadlines that are frequently unrealistic and therefore strongly counterproductive as far as the final objective of customer satisfaction is concerned. Managers often feel the pressure to produce zero-defect software, even though no one has ever done it. Productivity may be low; an inadequate process may have been inherited which has not been fixed and sufficiently automated, and it is difficult to know where to start. Against this background, testing practitioners and managers may well ask: "What do we do first?"

The answer is to start in the right place for your particular organization. Go for small gains. It isn't necessary to have all of Total Quality Management in place to make solid improvements in the development and testing processes. Before going any further, you should add some items to the potential improvement list (see Chapter 3 and Appendix H). Some possible inclusions derived from this chapter are listed below.

What can we do now?

Here are suggestions for items to include on your "clean sheet" described in Chapter 3.

- Discuss and obtain consensus on your organization's definition of testing. Use the definitions in this chapter as a starting point.
- When you next receive requirements, organize a meeting between the developers and testers to discuss them.
- Work for management support for more team spirit between testers and developers.

- Obtain management agreement that testing must begin early and that testing is not an after-the-fact activity.
- Obtain management agreement on proper staffing levels for testing each product.
- Invite a developer, or a manager of developers, to discuss product development risks.
- Plan a customer visit to discuss the ways the customer is going to use the product. This will provide ideas on how you should be testing the product.

References

Bender, R. (1993). "Writing testable requirements," *Software Testing Analysis & Review (STAR) Conference Proceedings*.

Hetzel, W. (1973). *Program Test Methods*. Englewood Cliffs, NJ: Prentice-Hall.

IEEE/ANSI (1983). IEEE Standard for Software Test Documentation, (Reaff. 1991), IEEE Std 829-1983.

IEEE/ANSI (1990). IEEE Standard Glossary of Software Engineering Terminology, IEEE Std 610.12-1990.

Myers, G.J. (1979). *The Art of Software Testing*. John Wiley.

Chapter 5
Critical choices: what, when, and how to test

Good testers are always capable of designing more tests than would ever be practical to implement and execute. Exhaustive testing would mean that many products never reach the market because testing would never be completed, and even if they did, they would be astronomically expensive.

Fifty per cent or more of the development organization's time is frequently devoted to error detection and removal, and in most organizations this massive use of resources is neither properly documented nor strategically justified. The real-world solution is to make choices, but on what should they be based?

One choice is to be sure we test the right things – to ensure the most critical items are tested and not to waste limited testing resources on less important items. Another choice is to test early – to focus on detecting the errors closer to the phase where they are introduced, in order to prevent the costly migration of errors downstream.

Testing has a life cycle that parallels the development cycle, one that includes both verification testing and validation testing. Testing processes should, as far as possible, be integrated at the most effective points in the development life cycle.

Testing resources can rarely be dramatically increased in the short term, so we have to use the ones we have in the best possible way.

Risk and risk management

Why would we hesitate before:

- making a parachute jump?
- using an experimental drug?
- investing $20,000 in the stock of a company?
- piloting a brand new aircraft on its initial flight?
- attempting to repair a high-voltage line?
- loaning a friend, or worse yet, a relative $10,000?

- disarming a bomb?
- hiring a teenager as a house sitter?

On the face of it, these undertakings are hazardous. They are risky. We need to work out how risky they are before we do them, and take all reasonable precautions against their coming out badly.

Risk is the probability that undesirable things will happen, such as loss of human life, or large financial losses. The systems we develop, when they don't work properly, have consequences that can vary from the mildly irritating to the catastrophic. Testing these systems should involve informed, conscious risk management.

We can't do everything. We have to make compromises, but we don't want to take risks that are unacceptably high. Key questions must be asked: "Who is going to use the product? What is it being used for? What is the danger of it going wrong? What are the consequences if it does? Is it loss of money? Is it a loss of customer satisfaction? Is it loss of life?"

For each product, we must implement the most cost-effective testing that will ensure that it's reliable enough, safe enough and meets the user/customer requirement. This may sound easy, but examples show that there can be hundreds of test cases for just a few lines of code. If every one of these cases took half a second to execute, it would still take decades to run all the possible test cases for a major product.

This doesn't mean we have to give up testing. It simply means that we never have enough time to test everything completely, so decisions have to be made based on the risks involved. When risk is used as a basis for testing choices, we are doing the rational thing and choosing the parts of the system that have the most serious consequences and focusing our attention on these.

Another basis for choice of testing focus is frequency of use. If a part of the system is used often, and it has an error in it, its frequent use alone makes the chances of a failure emerging much higher.

It is also rational to focus on those parts of the system or program that are most likely to have errors in them. There are many reasons why there may be extra risks involved in a particular piece of software, but the point is to look at them and make informed decisions based on that observation. The reason may be inherent in how that part of the system was created: it may be because the development team is constructed in a certain way and a junior person has written a complex piece of code, so that there's an extra risk in that part of the product; it could have to do with the schedule (too tight); it could have to do with the development resources (insufficient); it could have to do with the budget (too tight again).

In practice, this kind of risk analysis is often a matter of basic communication. If we talk to the development managers and product developers and ask what they are worried about, and their answer is: "Well, we've got an impossible schedule, and we have this very complex part of the system and we're not sure if we've got it right", then we as testers should treat this as an indication that we should give it special attention (see Figure 5.1).

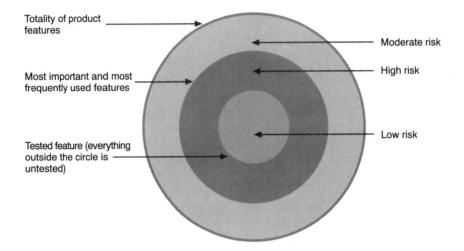

Figure 5.1   Risks in the system as a basis for testing choices. The key questions in this figure involve the "frequently used features." How accurately have they been identified? How close to reality are they? If they are close, then the relative proportions of risk may also be close. If they do not reflect reality, then the "high risk" area could be much larger than that shown. (© 1993, 1994 Software Development Technologies)

For each testing activity to be performed, testing objectives are prioritized by making judgments on the potential for all kinds of failure situations. Of 10 distinct testing activities (four in verification and six in validation – see Chapters 7 and 8), decisions must be made, based on the size, complexity and criticality of the product, about which activities (if any) may be skipped. In any event, we must aim to test to the degree that the risks are unacceptably high.

Risk is not just the basis for making management decisions on testing. It is the basis for decisions that test practitioners make every day. From Figure 5.1 it is clear that this is not a simple matter. But that doesn't mean that any attempt to assess the risk should be abandoned. Rather we should use the parameters spelled out in this section as a starting point for a more realistic assessment of the appropriateness of our present testing effort.

Start testing early

Each development phase (or translation) within the software development process creates a work product that can be tested to see how successful the translation is. At the early stages these work products are requirements and specifications, and they are available to be read and compared with other documents. Later in the process there is code that can be executed. It can, of course, also be reviewed on paper. If there is a choice, test early, because early is where many of the most important errors are, and this point is reinforced by the fact that more than 50% of all defects are usually introduced in the requirements stage alone.

Test early and prevent defect migration. Every time there is an opportunity to find a defect and we don't find it, and it is allowed to migrate to the next stage, it's going to cost much more to fix when we do find it. At the next stage, it can cost an order of magnitude more and an order of magnitude more again at the stage after that. The cost is maximized if the error is detected after the product is shipped to the customer and minimized if it's detected in the phase where it's introduced.

In the real world of projects under pressure and in a less than ideal organization, what can we do about poor requirements? They can be verified using the review methods in Chapter 7. Inspections can be started on a small scale. They have proven to be winners for more than 20 years in removing a high proportion of the errors. Even before proper verification is implemented, informal methods can help a lot.

Simple, better communication is one element. Customers change their minds about what they want. That is part of the process. But as testers and developers, we can be much more careful about how we record their requirements, how we review them and how we get agreement on them.

We can also facilitate the kind of communication that is so often missing by insisting on getting the right people to meet (product developers, customers, testers, and marketing) to talk about requirements and specifications, and record them meticulously. Often much of this communication will be about language and defining terms: "This is the deliverable, and this is who is responsible for that deliverable, and this is how we change that deliverable, and as it's critical, this is how we are going to test it." At this point, we are starting to touch base with the real software engineering process and maturity issues.

Basic forms of the testing process – verification and validation

Testing can be separated into two basic forms. Given the value of testing early, these definitions of testing are not only confined to testing code, but also include the testing of documents and other non-executable forms of a product.

> *Verification,* as defined by IEEE/ANSI, is the process of evaluating a system or component to determine whether the products of a given development phase satisfy the conditions imposed at the start of that phase.

Do we have clear and complete requirements? Is there a good design, and what are the work products produced in the design? Verification is the process of evaluating, reviewing, inspecting, and doing desk checks of work products such as requirement specifications, design specifications, and code. For code it means the static analysis of the code – a code review – not the dynamic execution of the code. Verification testing can be applied to all those things that can be reviewed in the early phases to make sure that what comes out of that phase is what we expected to get.

Some people call verification "human" testing, because it usually involves looking at documents on paper. By contrast, validation usually involves the execution of software on a computer.

Validation, as defined by IEEE/ANSI, is the process of evaluating a system or component during or at the end of the development process to determine whether it satisfies specified requirements.

Validation normally involves executing the actual software or a simulated mock-up. Validation is a "computer-based testing" process. It usually exposes symptoms of errors.

It is a central thesis of this book that testing includes both verification and validation.

Definition: Testing = verification plus validation

Verification and validation are complementary. The effectiveness of error detection suffers if one or the other is not done. Each of them provides filters that are designed to catch different kinds of problems in the product.

Historically testing has been, and continues to be, largely validation-orientated. It is not that we should stop doing validation, but we want to be a lot smarter about how we do it, and how we do it in combination with verification. We must also ensure that we do each of them at the right time on the right work products.

Testing, the development cycle, and the real world of contracts

Depending on the type of organization and other circumstances, there are variations to the software life-cycle model, but they all have much in common. Figure 5.2 shows a typical model for the development life cycle and the place of testing within it.

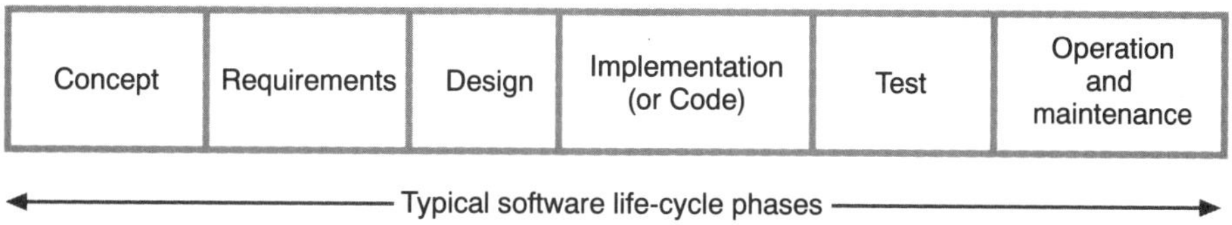

Concept	Requirements	Design	Implementation (or Code)	Test	Operation and maintenance

← ———————————— Typical software life-cycle phases ———————————— →

Figure 5.2 Software development process overview. This is a typical model for the development life cycle. IEEE/ANSI Software Verification and Validation Plans (Standard 1012-1986) has another phase called "installation and checkout" between "test" and "operation and maintenance." IEEE/ANSI does not require a specific model. (© 1993, 1994 Software Development Technologies)

The "test" phase is named primarily for historical reasons, and is the period of time in the life cycle in which the components of the software product are evaluated and integrated, and the validation tests are executed. The design phase is often divided into functional design and internal design.

Developing software life-cycle processes – IEEE/ANSI, 1991 (Std 1074-1991)

This standard defines the set of activities that constitute the processes that are mandatory for the development and maintenance of software. The management and support processes that continue throughout the entire life cycle, as well as all aspects of the software life cycle from concept exploration through retirement, are covered. Associated input and output information are also provided. Utilization of the processes and their component activities maximizes the benefits to the user when the use of this standard is initiated early in the software life cycle. This standard requires the definition of a user's software life cycle and shows its mapping into typical software life cycles. It is not intended to define or imply a specific software life cycle of its own.

There are variations on each of these life-cycle models. They all raise some important organizational questions: "Who really does the testing? Is the testing subcontracted as well? Is it given to the same contractor who is doing the development?" The main point is that there are phases, and for each development phase, there is a corresponding phase for testing.

The Dotted-U Model in Figure 5.3 shows in more detail the integration of the development cycle and the testing cycle.

Note the one-to-one correspondence between development and test phases in their respective cycles. Each major deliverable produced by development is tested (verified or validated) by the testing organization. In the development life cycle there is a requirements phase and in the testing life cycle there is a requirements verification phase. Design verification goes along with the design development phase, and so on. Note that the planning

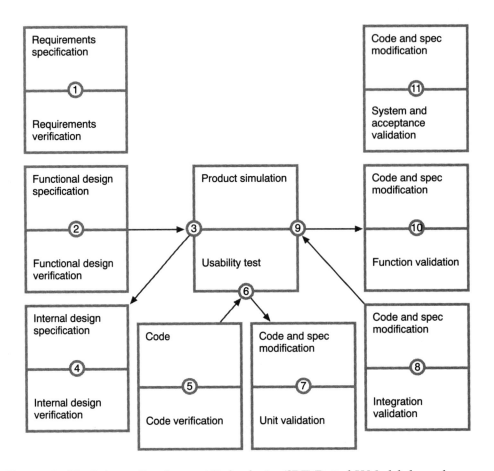

Figure 5.3   The Software Development Technologies (SDT) Dotted-U Model above shows the integration of the development and the test process. This book clearly describes all of the components shown in the model. (© 1993, 1994 Software Development Technologies)

for any testing activity may occur before that activity is depicted in the figure. Each of the 10 fundamental testing activities shown (four in verification and six in validation) is covered in detail.

Effective testing ...

Effective testing removes errors. In any particular case, how do we know how much testing we should aim to do? Should we do full testing or only partial testing?

The basic forms of testing are as follows:

(1) *Full testing* starts no later than the requirements phase, and continues through acceptance testing.
(2) *Partial testing* begins any time after functional design has been completed, with less than optimal influence on requirements and functional design.
(3) *Endgame testing* is highly validation orientated, with no influence on requirements or functional design.
(4) *Audit-level testing* is a bare-bones audit of plans, procedures, and products for adequacy, correctness, and compliance to standards. (Lewis, 1992)

Once again, a big part of the answer lies in risk management. To make effective risk management decisions, we need a clear definition for critical software.

> *Critical software*, as defined by IEEE/ANSI (1990 [Std 610.12-1990]), is software whose failure could have an impact on safety, or could cause large financial or social losses.

Use full testing for critical software or any software that will have heavy and diverse usage by a large user population.

Use partial testing for small, non-critical software products with a small, captive user population (i.e., where the consequences of failures are never damaging).

To enable an effective test effort, we need a software development process that produces:

- *requirements specifications* (required for full testing);
- *functional design specifications* (required for full, partial, and endgame testing);
- *internal design specifications* (required for maximum effectiveness of full and partial testing).

From a testing perspective, full testing means we must have reasonably clear and complete requirements specifications. One of the first things testers can do to improve their process is to press for access to the kind of specification that they need.

For partial or endgame testing we need at least the functional design specifications. For maximum effectiveness we need the internal design specifications because internal information of this kind tells us how the product has been constructed.

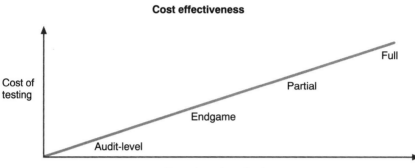

Figure 5.4   The more effective the error detection, the greater the savings in development and maintenance costs over the life of the product. (© 1993, 1994 Software Development Technologies)

... and cost-effective testing

Effective testing is testing that is successful at detecting errors. But this may not be an exercise that is always worthwhile from a financial point of view. We have considered the cost of errors (what they cost if they remain in the product), but in a real-world environment we need to confront and make explicit a number of questions about the cost effectiveness of our testing effort.

Do we know what testing is really costing us? How is it affecting development time? Do we know what percentage of our development resource testing represents? Are testing tools saving us time? Are they paying for themselves? Are we trained to exploit them to the full, or have they already become shelfware? Are we using our testing resources to find errors that represent the biggest financial risk? If we look at the overall impact on our business objectives of testing the products of our development, is our testing cost effective? (See Figure 5.4.)

When we start to ask these kinds of questions within real-world organizations, we find the gulf between awareness and action to be very wide indeed. In other words, many people are aware they ought to know the answers to these questions, but they know that they are far away from doing so, usually because they are too busy fighting today's fires.

Frequently, they believe that these kinds of questions are management's problem, as indeed they are. In practice, questions of the cost effectiveness of the testing process rarely get considered. (For more detail on cost effectiveness and its measurement, see Chapter 12.)

"The more effective the error detection, the greater the savings in development and maintenance costs over the life of the product. Several examples have indicated that partial testing can yield a saving of 1.5 times its cost; full testing can yield savings of up to 2 times its cost. Whether or not there is universal agreement that these numbers are totally accurate does not matter as much as the fact that they substantiate the premise that testing can invariably pay for itself."

(Lewis, 1992: p. 280)

What can we do now?

- Start to make a risk assessment based on the factors in this chapter most relevant to your environment.
- Evaluate whether you have the appropriate mix between partial and full testing.
- Talk to developers about areas of the system they are worried about (even if it's just on a "gut feeling" level).
- Get developers, testers, and preferably also customers and marketing people together to improve requirements specifications.
- Evaluate the gains in your organization from doing more (early) verification testing.

References

IEEE/ANSI (1986). IEEE Standard for Software Verification and Validation Plans, (Reaff. 1992), IEEE Std 1012-1986.

IEEE/ANSI (1990). IEEE Standard Glossary of Software Engineering Terminology, IEEE Std 610.12-1990.

IEEE/ANSI (1991). IEEE Standard for Developing Software Life Cycle Processes, IEEE Std 1074-1991.

Lewis, R. (1992). *Independent Verification and Validation*. John Wiley.

Chapter 6
Critical disciplines: frameworks for testing

Any software engineering method that is common practice in software development projects is usually also applicable to software testing efforts. This means that the disciplines of planning and analysis, formal documents, configuration management, measurement, standards, tools, and procedures can be applied to testing.

As projects become more complex, and development and testing groups become larger, these disciplines become increasingly critical to success.

Most of these ideas come together in the notion of *process maturity*. The more of these disciplines we are doing, and the more we are doing systematically, the more mature our software process. Most of them are handled in greater detail later in the book.

Planning

Without a plan, we don't know:

- what we're going to do
- how we're going to do it
- how long it will take
- the resources required
- the cost.

It is easy to see why medium-sized (let alone large) software development projects become so disastrously out of control if the planning is not done properly. Planning is the first step of every testing activity.

If testing is to be included as a serious part of software engineering, testers have to take time to analyze the product. Product requirements must be reviewed before tests are designed. Tests should be designed before implementation is started. In fact, the process of designing tests helps to detect specification defects. Specifications are therefore improved by a good testing process. In other words, we have to plan, and once we start planning, all kinds of other questions come up.

What kinds of standards are going to be useful? Are we going to do to inspections and reviews? What kinds of tools should we be using to find the most critical problems in this particular product? Do we have the time and financial resources to cover the testing we have to do? What kind of review are we going to have of our processes as testers? Do we have our priorities right?

There is a general human tendency to want to "get on with the next thing," especially under time pressure. For testers this usually means working the code and finding errors in it. However, resources spent intelligently on the earlier testing phases are repaid many times over. Time spent on early planning is never wasted, and usually the total time cycle is significantly shorter. There are two distinct stages, planning and execution, of each activity within verification. This is the case regardless of whether we are doing requirements verification, functional design verification, internal design verification, or code verification.

The considerations in verification planning

For each type of verification (requirements, functional design, internal design, code) the issues to be addressed are as follows:

- the verification activity to be performed;
- the methods used (inspection, walkthrough, etc.);
- the specific areas of the work product that will and will not be verified;
- the risks associated with any areas that will not be verified;
- prioritizing the areas of the work product to be verified;
- resources, schedule, facilities, tools, and responsibilities.

The considerations in validation planning

Validation testing activities include unit testing (by development), integration testing (by development), usability testing, function testing, system testing, and acceptance testing. The tasks associated with this are high-level planning for all validation activities as a whole and testware architectural design.

For each validation activity we have to do:

- detailed planning
- testware design and development
- test execution
- test evaluation
- testware maintenance.

For validation planning the issues to be addressed are as follows:

- test methods
- facilities (for testware development vs. test execution)
- test automation
- testing tools
- support software (shared by development and test)
- configuration management
- risks (budget, resources, schedule, training).

(There is more detail on planning and master test plans in Chapter 10.)

Software engineering maturity and the SEI

The Software Engineering Institute (SEI) is a federally-funded research and development center, sponsored by the Department of Defense, and affiliated with Carnegie Mellon University. It was established by Congress in 1984 to address a twofold shortage of trained software professionals and quality software, produced on schedule and within budget.

The mission of the SEI is to provide leadership to advance the state-of-the-practice of software engineering to improve the quality of systems that depend on software. The SEI focuses on software process, on the assumption that improving the process, which means bringing engineering discipline to the development and maintenance of software, is the key to better quality software products. This is consistent with the basic premise of this book – the importance of the software testing process.

SEI process maturity levels

To assess the ability of development organizations to develop software in accordance with modern software engineering methods, the SEI defines five process maturity levels as part of a process model called the Capability Maturity Model (CMM):

Level 1: *Initial*	(Anarchy)	Unpredictable and poorly controlled
Level 2: *Repeatable*	(Folklore)	Can repeat previously mastered tasks
Level 3: *Defined*	(Standards)	Process characterized, fairly well understood
Level 4: *Managed*	(Measurement)	Process measured and controlled
Level 5: *Optimizing*	(Optimization)	Focus on process improvement

Few organizations are beyond level 1 on the maturity scale, which is characterized as consisting of unpredictable, poorly-controlled processes. To achieve level 2, previously mastered tasks have to be repeatable. In other words, we have the disciplines in place for proper project control, project planning, reviews, and communication control.

While general software process improvement and maturity are beyond the scope of what many testers do every day, the SEI CMM describes goals and activities that are of vital importance to anyone striving to improve their everyday testing process. In fact, activities associated with level 3 that specifically relate to testing include the following:

Level 3, Activity 5: Software testing is performed according to the project's defined software process

(1) Testing criteria are developed and reviewed with the customer and the end user, as appropriate.

(2) Effective methods are used to test the software.

(3) The adequacy of testing is determined by:
   (i)   the level of testing performed (e.g., unit testing, integration testing, system testing),
   (ii) the test strategy selected (e.g., black-box, white-box), and
   (iii) the test coverage to be achieved (e.g., statement coverage, branch coverage).

(4) For each level of software testing, test readiness criteria are established and used.

(5) Regression testing is performed, as appropriate, at each test level whenever the software being tested or its environment changes.

(6) The test plans, test procedures, and test cases undergo peer review before they are considered ready for use.

(7) The test plans, test procedures, and test cases are managed and controlled (e.g., placed under configuration management).

(8) Test plans, test procedures, and test cases are appropriately changed whenever the allocated requirements, software requirements, software design, or code being tested changes.

Level 3, Activity 6: Integration testing of the software is planned and performed according to the project's defined software process

(1) The plans for integration testing are documented and based on the software development plan.

(2) The integration test cases and test procedures are reviewed with the individuals responsible for the software requirements, software design, and system and acceptance testing.

(3) Integration testing of the software is performed against the designated version of the software requirements document and the software design document.

Level 3, Activity 7: System and acceptance testing of the software are planned and performed to demonstrate that the software satisfies its requirements

(1) Resources for testing the software are assigned early enough to provide for adequate test preparation.

(2) System and acceptance testing are documented in a test plan, which is reviewed with, and approved by, the customer and end users, as appropriate.

(3) The test cases and test procedures are planned and prepared by a test group that is independent of the software developers.

(4) The test cases are documented and are reviewed with, and approved by, the customer and end users, as appropriate, before the testing begins.

(5) Testing of the software is perfomed against baselined software and the baselined documentation of the allocated requirements and the software requirements.

(6) Problems identified during testing are documented and tracked to closure.

(7) Test results are documented and used as the basis for determining whether the software satisfies its requirements.

(8) The test results are managed and controlled.

How process maturity affects testing

There are strong indications that the amount of testing budget spent on non-technical (management) issues is in inverse proportion to the maturity level within the environment as a whole (see Figure 6.1).

Level 1 organizations are characterized by so much uncertainty that the outcome is unpredictable. To the extent that development doesn't know where it is going, testing cannot plan its own activities and will spend more time working on non-technical issues.

There are special consultancy service organizations trained in the SEI model which conduct software process assessments (SPAs) on request. SPA is a method developed by the SEI to help organizations evaluate their software process maturity and identify key areas for improvement. They look at the practices an organization is using and recommend practices that should be implemented now to improve processes.

SPA is based on a series of questions specific to particular subject areas, and a number of follow-up questions that expand on the information obtained. Answers are weighted according to the importance of their subject matter (see Humphrey, 1989).

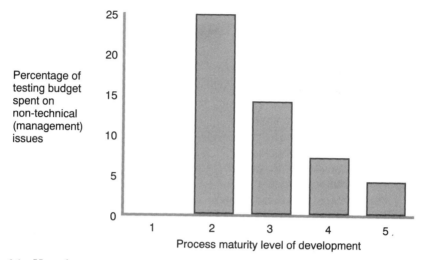

Figure 6.1   How the process maturity level affects testing (Lewis, 1992). To the extent that development doesn't know where it is going, testing cannot plan its own activities and will spend more time on management issues rather than technical issues. (© 1993, 1994 Software Development Technologies)

More detail on SEI assessment

SEI evaluation questions are divided into seven sections. The following sample questions all apply to organizations at Level 1 which are aiming for Level 2.

Organization:
Is there a software configuration control function for each project that involves software development?

Resources, personnel, and training:
Is there is a required training program for all newly appointed development managers designed to familiarize them with software project management?

Technology management:
Is a mechanism used for maintaining awareness of the state of the art in software engineering technologies?

Documented standards and procedures:
Is a formal procedure used in the management review of each software development prior to making contractual commitments?

Process metrics:
Are software staffing profiles maintained of actual staffing versus planned staffing?

Data management and analysis:
Is review efficiency analyzed for each project? (level 4 question)

Process control:
Is a mechanism used for controlling changes to the software requirements?

Configuration management

Configuration management (CM) problems stem from confusion and lack of control. These problems can waste enormous amounts of time; they often happen at the worst possible moment; they are almost always very frustrating, and they are totally unnecessary.

If...
... we can't identify the source code that corresponds to a given module of object code;
... we can't determine which version of the COBOL compiler generated a given object module;
... a bug that was corrected last month suddenly reappears;
... we can't identify the source-code changes that were made in a particular revision of software;
... simultaneous changes are made to the same source module by multiple developers, and some of the changes are lost;
... shared (source) code is changed, and all programmers sharing the code are not notified;
... changes are made to the interface of common (runtime) code, and all users are not notified;
... changes are made, and the changes are not propagated to all affected versions (releases) of the code...
... then what is lacking is configuration management.

What is CM?

Configuration management (CM) is a four-part discipline applying technical and administrative direction, control, and surveillance for:

(1) *Configuration identification*
  (i)   conventions for identifying baseline and revision levels for all program files (source, object listing) and revision-specific documents;
  (ii) derivation records identify "build" participants (including source and object files, tools and revision levels used, data files).
(2) *Configuration and change control*
  (i)   safeguard defined and approved baselines;
  (ii) prevent unnecessary or marginal changes;
  (iii) expedite worthwhile changes.
(3) *Configuration status accounting*
  (i)   recording and tracking problem reports, change requests, change orders, etc.

(4) *Configuration audit*
   (i) unscheduled audits for standards compliance;
   (ii) scheduled functional and physical audits near the end of the project.

CM is the key to managing and coordinating changes (see Figure 6.2). It is essential for software projects with more than a few people, and with more than a modest change volume. It is a simple concept, but is often complex in its detailed practice. It is applicable to and critically important for programs as well as tests and data, and for code as well as all preceding life-cycle documents in the derivation path of the code.

CM answers questions like the following:

- What is our current software configuration?
- What is its status?
- How do we control changes to our configuration?
- What changes have been made to our software?
- Do anyone else's changes affect our software?

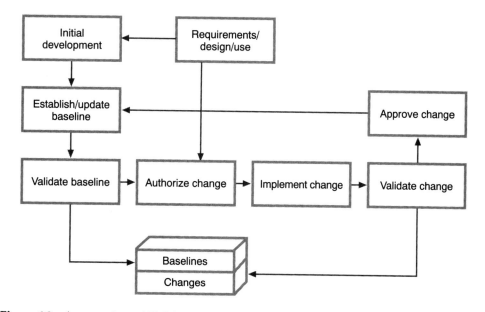

Figure 6.2 An overview of CM. (© 1993, 1994 Software Development Technologies)

Testing's interest in CM

Testing's interest in CM consists of the following concerns:

- to manage its own validation tests and their revision levels efficiently;
- to associate a given version of a test with the appropriate version of the software to be tested;
- to ensure that problem reports can identify software and hardware configurations accurately;
- to ensure that the right thing is built by development;
- to ensure that the right thing is tested;
- to ensure that the right thing is shipped to the customer.

The testing interest is important because we want to make sure several things are happening: Are we testing the right thing? From whom are we getting the thing we're testing? How do we know that if we test it, and it's okay, that that's the thing that gets shipped to the customer? How do we control changes to it? When do we let people change things and where do they change them? How do we make sure that we change them in a way that isn't going to have negative effects? Who is controlling it? These are all CM questions (see Beresoff, 1980; Humphrey, 1989; IEEE/ANSI, 1987 [Std 1042-1987], 1990 [Std 828-1990).

There are entire courses and books on configuration management. The basic activity is to identify the components that matter in the system and track their status. It is important that this is not an *ad hoc* matter, but is seen as a discipline to be applied with its own guidelines and which becomes part of "how we do things in this organization" lore – initiated, maintained, upgraded, and improved along with other practices that contribute to process maturity.

Standards

Why standards? The use of standards simplifies communication, promotes consistency and uniformity, and eliminates the need to invent yet another (often different and even incompatible) solution to the same problem. Standards, whether "official" or merely agreed upon, are especially important when we're talking to customers and suppliers, but it's easy to underestimate their importance when dealing with different departments and disciplines within our own organization. They also provide vital continuity so that we are not forever reinventing the wheel. They are a way of preserving proven practices above and beyond the inevitable staff changes within organizations.

Some standards are particularly important to the testing practitioner. They can provide a benchmark for writing documents like requirements, so that testers and others doing verification have a framework for what they can expect to find. More specifically, standards tell us what to put into key test documents, such as a test plan.

Standards are not only practical from the development point of view, but they are increasingly the basis for contracts and therefore also, when things go wrong, for litigation. One of the issues that arises in litigation is whether the software was developed according to known standards that are prevalent in the industry today. This means we need to know not only what the standards are, but to also see that they are applied.

IEEE/ANSI standards

Many key standards relating to software testing are generated by the Institute of Electrical and Electronics Engineers (IEEE). A transnational organization founded in 1884, IEEE consists of dozens of specialized societies within geographical regions throughout the world. Software testing standards are developed within the Technical Committees of the IEEE Societies and the Standards Coordinating Committees of the IEEE Standards Board.

These standards are created through a process of obtaining the consensus of practicing professionals. This consensus process, which includes careful discussion and debate among members of the various committees who serve voluntarily, is one of the fundamental themes of the standards process. Another key theme is to provide standards in a timely manner; from project approval to standard approval is approximately three years.

Key US software testing standards

- IEEE Standard for Software Test Documentation, Reaff. 1991 (IEEE/ANSI Std 829-1983)
- IEEE Standard for Software Unit Testing, Reaff. 1993 (IEEE/ANSI Std 1008-1987)

Other standards related to software testing

- IEEE Standard for Software Verification and Validation Plans, Reaff. 1992 (IEEE/ANSI Std 1012-1986)
- IEEE Standard for Software Reviews and Audits (IEEE/ANSI Std 1028-1988)
- IEEE Standard for Software Quality Assurance Plans (IEEE/ANSI Std 730-1989)
- IEEE Standard Glossary of Software Engineering Terminology (IEEE/ANSI Std 610.12-1990)

One of the earliest and perhaps still the most important software testing standard, the Standard for Software Test Documentation was initially approved by IEEE in 1982 and by ANSI in 1983, and was reaffirmed in 1991. This standard describes the content and format of basic software testing documents. It is often the first standard to be used by test practitioners as the basis and template for key test documents such as test plans, test design specifications, and test summary reports.

The other key standard, the Standard for Software Unit Testing, specifies a systematic approach to software unit testing and provides guidance to assist with the implementation and usage of unit testing. The standard describes a testing process composed of a hierarchy of phases, activities, and tasks. It defines a minimum set of tasks for each activity.

IEEE uses one of three designations in every document title:

(1) *Standard* means "must use";

(2) *Recommended practice* means "should use";

(3) *Guide* means "use at your discretion".

These standards provide recommendations reflecting the state of the practice in software testing. Think of it as receiving extremely cost-effective advice from concerned professionals who have thought long and hard about key issues facing those both new and old to software engineering.

Once approved by IEEE, many of these standards go on to be approved as American National Standards Institute (ANSI) standards. It is the coordinator of America's voluntary standards system. ANSI will approve standards as American National Standards after it has verified evidence that consensus exists. ANSI verifies that all substantially affected interests have been given an opportunity to participate in the development of a standard or to comment on its provisions and that their views have been carefully considered.

More detail on US standards

The IEEE/ANSI software engineering standards can be purchased through IEEE.

Contact for IEEE:
IEEE
445 Hoes Lane
PO Box 1331
Piscataway, NJ 08855-1331 USA
Freephone: (1) 800 678 IEEE
From outside USA: (1) 908 981 0060

Two primary subcommittees of the IEEE Computer Society that deal with software engineering:

(1) Software Engineering Standards Subcommittee (SESS) which approves and reaffirms software engineering standards

(2) Technical Committee on Software Engineering (TCSE)

Contact for both is:
Elliot Chikofsky
PO Box 400
Burlington, MA 01803 USA

The evolution of software engineering standards is far from over. Existing standards are reviewed at least once every five years, and new standards are always in process.

ISO 9000, SPICE and other standards

The ISO 9000 series of standards addresses the quality management system of an organization, and ISO 9001 is the base international standard for quality management. ISO 9000-3 is a guidebook on how ISO 9001 applies to software. TickIt is a UK scheme for certifying organizations producing software according to ISO 9001.

As different sectors in different countries have focused on different standards, there has been concern that individual organizations could find that they operate as a trade restraint rather than a promoter of successful international cooperation. A company might improve its processes to acquire certification by one model only to find that new markets require evaluation according to another. Others have expressed concern that ISO 9000 has little to do with achieving product quality and is rarely utilized as a means for software process improvement.

An important working group of the International Organization for Standards (ISO), unrelated to ISO 9000, is WG10: Software Process Assessment. This group has established a project called "Software Process Improvement and Capability Determination" (SPICE) to develop a suite of related standards and guidebooks. The purpose is to create a consistent standard for software process assessment that can be used by different nations and different sectors. The Software Engineering Institute has worked closely with this working group, including providing the Capability Maturity Model as input to the ISO effort.

More detail on other standards

Contact for the SPICE initiative:
Software Engineering Institute
Carnegie Mellon University
Pittsburgh, PA 15213-3890
Tel: (1) 412 268 5813

Published British Standards cross-referenced to their International counterparts are listed in the British Standards Institute's "Standards Catalogue".

Contact:
British Standards Institute (BSI)
Linford Wood
Milton Keynes MK14 6LE
Tel: (44) 1908 221 166

Appendix A of this book lists all the current IEEE/ANSI standards that are relevant to software engineering and a short review of each one, as well as further details on ISO 9000 and SPICE publications.

Formal documents

While the developer's (and tester's) worst nightmare may be paperwork, it has proven to be an absolutely essential element of any successful project. A formal document is a document of which the form, general content, and timing has been agreed in advance. It is a deliverable.

We need documents in order to put decisions in writing. The act of writing requires hundreds of mini-decisions, each of which helps to distinguish clear thoughts from fuzzy ones. Documents also provide a vehicle for communicating information to others, and they help to communicate that information consistently. Documents delivered by the development and testing groups provide essential input to management, in a form that management can understand and handle.

Each phase of the software life cycle calls for one or more deliverables in the form of documents. Apart from the code, development has three major deliverables in the form of documents:

(1) *Requirements specification.* Don't discard these after their initial approval. Some organizations do.

(2) *Functional design specification.* Don't discard the functional design specification and start relying on user manuals as the definitive description of the external interfaces. Some organizations do.

(3) *Internal design specification.* Insist that development produce an internal design specification. Some organizations don't.

A mature development organization will produce these documents and faithfully maintain them for the life of the product. With proper configuration management, any change is reflected in all affected documents. These documents are under change control and kept in lockstep with the code.

Testing produces its own formal documents corresponding to its own life cycle, and these form part of testware.

Testware

A deliverable is a major work product of an organization. Hardware development engineers produce hardware. Software development engineers produce software. Software test engineers produce testware.

Testware is produced by both verification and validation testing methods. Testware includes verification checklists, verification error statistics, test data, and supporting documentation like test plans, test specifications, test procedures, test cases, test data, and test reports.

Testware is so named because it has a life beyond its initial use. Like software, it should be placed under the control of a configuration management system, saved, and faithfully maintained. Contrary to popular perception, testing is not an on-the-fly activity with no tangible remains when the work is complete. Like software, testware has significant value because it can be reused without incurring the cost of redevelopment with each use.

It is important to maintain testware, just as software and hardware are maintained. Part of the tester's job is to create testware that is going to have a specified lifetime and is a valuable asset to the company, controlled and managed like any other. When testware is being created, it has to be put under some kind of control so that it is not lost. If a particular tester leaves the company, someone else can then maintain and continue the process.

Giving testware a name helps to give validity to a test organization that doesn't usually think in terms of having a specific deliverable. It gives ownership to what testers do. Professional testers have a product. Testers have test libraries, their own code and their own software. Testers' specific deliverables are testware. The concept of testware can make it easier for testers to communicate with each other and with other organizations.

Testware is referred to throughout this book. Testware management, though not directly related to error detection, has an enormous impact on the efficiency of the test effort. There is more detail on verification testware in Chapter 7, and on testing deliverables at each phase of the life cycle and the management of testware in Chapter 9.

Measurement

Without measurements, we never know whether we're moving forward or backward or standing still. It is no coincidence that a major section of the SEI Software Process Assessment questionnaire is devoted to process metrics.

Sample process metrics questions

- Are statistics of software errors gathered?
- Are profiles maintained of actual versus planned test cases for groups completing testing?
- Are software trouble reports resulting from testing tracked to closure?
- Are design and code review coverage measured and recorded?

Mature development and testing organizations are able to provide metrics on all key elements in their process. This is not only because they need to monitor their performance, their use of resources and their efficiency as a basis for management decisions, but also because even asking the questions relating to collecting the statistics is a major springboard for process improvement, at any level.

While measurement can easily look like more unnecessary bureaucracy, there are a number of big questions for testing to which the development of measures within the organization is the only way to get answers, and thus make good decisions in the future.

Measurement can tell us …

- What was the (real) size of the test effort on a given product?
- How efficient were our verification efforts?
- How thorough were our validation tests?
- What was the quality of the product:
  - during test (before customer use)?
  - in production use by customers?
  - compared to other products?
- How many (approximately) errors are there in the product:
  - before testing begins?
  - later, after some experience with the product?
- When do we stop testing?

Measurement provides an idea of the real program complexity. It helps in planning the test effort, and in predicting how many errors there are and where they occur. Measurement of the number and types of errors detected provides an accurate idea of our efficiency at verification and the weaknesses in our development process.

Measuring validation test coverage provides quantitative assessments of the thoroughness and comprehensiveness of our validation tests. Tracking test execution status monitors the convergence of test categories and provides quantitative information on when to stop testing.

Measuring and tracking incident reports (by severity category):

- provides a leading indicator of product quality;
- provides significant criteria for release readiness;
- correlates to users' satisfaction with the product;
- serves as a predictor of the number of remaining errors;
- when normalized, provides a measure of product quality relative to other products;
- provides a measure of testing efficiency (customer reported vs. testing reported incidents).

Remember that

"You can't control what you can't measure."

Tom DeMarco, 1982

(See Chapter 12 for more details on useful measures and how to implement them.)

Tools

Testing tools, like any other kinds of tools, provide leverage. There is a wide variety of tools available today to provide assistance in every phase of the testing process. If we are to maximize the benefit we get from tools, there are a number of questions to be asked as part of implementing an effective tools program:

(1) How do the tools fit into and support our test process?
(2) Do we know how to plan and design tests? (Tools do not eliminate the need to think, to plan, and to design.)
(3) Who will be responsible for making sure we get the proper training on our new tool?
(4) Who will promote and support tool use within the organization on an ongoing basis?

In other words, like all testing activities, the use of tools needs to be integrated with the larger picture of our development process.

"Simply throwing a tool at a testing problem will not make it go away."
Dorothy Graham, *The CAST Report*

Tools can be categorized in a number of ways:

- by the testing activity or task in which they are employed (e.g., code verification, test planning, test execution);
- by descriptive functional keyword, in other words the specific function performed by the tool (e.g., capture/reply, logic coverage, comparator);
- by major areas of classification, in other words a small number of high-level classes or groupings of tools, each class containing tools that are similar in function or other characteristic (e.g., test management, static analysis, simulator).

For the purposes of this book, and in order to emphasize that testing has a life cycle of its own, these tools will be discussed in Chapter 11 under the following headings:

- reviews and inspections
- test planning
- test design and development
- test execution and evaluation
- test support.

There is a critical gap between awareness of these tools and effective action in evaluating, selecting, and implementing them. Whatever the level of maturity of the development process, a proper strategy for tool selection and evaluation is essential. (See Chapter 11 for detailed material on tools, their categorization, their acquisition, and implementation.)

What can we do now?

- Raise awareness of standards within your organization. Get copies of one or two key ones. Start with the standard for Software Test Documentation. Demonstrate the benefits of using this standard to assist with writing test plans.
- Make some preliminary evaluations of how you are using tools in your organization. Do you know whether you are doing as well as you might? Access at least one sound objective source of expert advice on tools.

- Obtain a set of SEI Maturity Assessment questions and apply a limited set of them to the relevant part of your organization. Even asking the questions is helpful. It will demonstrate very vividly where you are – and how urgent it is that you start to get some of these disciplines in place. Consider getting independent help from a consultant specializing in process assessment.
- Raise awareness of testware in your organization. It is a capital asset, to be recognized, nurtured, maintained, and expanded. Get management support for testware.
- Find out more about configuration management. Is someone responsible for this in your organization? If it isn't formally implemented, start to use it informally within your own area. Demonstrate the benefits to a wider group.

References

Beresoff, E.H., Henderson, V. D. and Siegel, S.G. (1980). "Software configuration management: a tutorial," *IEEE Tutorial: Software Configuration Management*, IEEE Cat. No. EHO 169-3, 27 October, 24–32.

DeMarco, T. (1982). *Controlling Software Projects*. Yourdon Press.

Humphrey, W.S. (1989). *Managing the Software Process*. Reading, MA: Addison-Wesley.

IEEE/ANSI (1987). IEEE Guide to Software Configuration Management, (Reaff. 1993), IEEE Std 1042-1987.

IEEE/ANSI (1990). IEEE Standard for Software Configuration Management Plans, IEEE Std 828-1990.

The clearing house of Computer Science Technical Reports and source of SEI technical reports is:
Research Access Inc.
3400 Forbes Ave., Suite 302
Pittsburgh, PA 15213
Tel. (1) 800 685 6510

See also:
Software Engineering Institute, Tel. (1) 412 268 7700

PART III
Testing methods

"It is very dangerous to try and leap a chasm in two bounds."

CHINESE PROVERB

Chapter 7
Verification testing

Chapter 8
Validation testing

Chapter 9
Controlling validation costs

Chapter 10
Testing tasks, deliverables, and chronology

Chapter 11
Software testing tools

Chapter 12
Measurement

Chapter 7
Verification testing

Each verification activity is a phase of the testing life cycle. The testing objective in each verification activity is to detect as many errors as possible. The testing team should leverage its efforts by participating in any inspections and walkthroughs conducted by development and by initiating verification, especially at the early stages of development.

In addition, the testing team should develop its own verification "testware" in the form of generic and testing-specific checklists for all kinds of documents, so that verification expertise becomes an asset of the organization. The testware itself, like all other software, should also be verified.

Testing should use verification practices as a springboard for improving interdisciplinary communication about essential matters as well as promoting the general maturity of the development environment.

You should do as much and as thorough a verification as possible. It has proven to be one of the surest and most cost-effective routes to quality improvement in both the short and the long term.

Basic verification methods

Verification is a "human" examination or review of the work product. There are various types of reviews. Inspections, walkthroughs, technical reviews and other methods are not always referred to consistently, but inspections are generally considered the most formal.

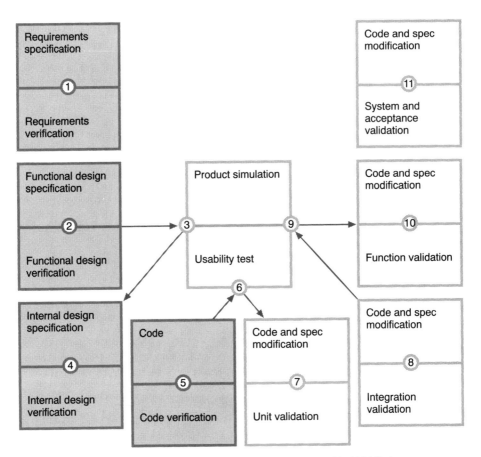

Figure 7.1   The SDT Dotted-U Model, verification testing. (© 1993, 1994 Software Development Technologies)

Basic features of verification methods

	Inspections	**Walkthroughs**	**Buddy checks**
Presenter	not author	anyone	none
Participants	team 3–6	larger numbers	1 or 2
Preparation	yes	presenter only	none
Data collected	yes	not required	none
Output report	yes	not required	verbal comment
Advantages	effective	familiarizes larger numbers	inexpensive to do
Disadvantages	short-term cost	finds fewer errors	finds fewer errors

Formal structured types of verification

Formal reviews, technical reviews, and inspections are various expressions used for the more structured types of verification. In the following sections we shall refer mostly to inspections, simply because they are the most structured, but this does not imply the exclusion of the other methods or that we question their value.

The central "event" in these methods is a meeting at which defects in the product under review are discussed and discovered.

Formal methods – key elements

(1) Everyone in the review group participates openly and actively, and participation is governed by traditions, customs and written rules about how such a review is to be conducted.

(2) A written report is produced regarding the status of the product, and the report is available to everyone involved in the project, including management.

(3) The review group is responsible for the quality of information in the written report.

(Freedman and Weinberg, 1990)

Inspections are also characterized by individual preparation by all participants prior to the meeting. Participants are told by the inspection team leader what their reviewer role is, i.e., from what point of view to read the material. When performing inspections well, most of the total defects to be discovered are found during preparation, though an effective inspection meeting will usually uncover some significant additional defects.

Inspection: key elements and phases

Objectives:
- to obtain defects and collect data; meeting does not examine alternative solutions;
- to communicate important work product information.

Elements:
- a planned, structured meeting requiring individual preparation by all participants;
- a team of 3–6 people, led by an impartial moderator;
- presenter is "reader" other than the producer.

Input:
- document to be inspected;
- related source documents;
- general and "tailored" checklists.

Output:
- inspection summary/report;
- data on error types.

Key phases:
- briefing/entry – individual preparation – inspection meeting – edit/rework – exit/re-inspect – collect data;
- some versions of inspection include causal analysis meetings.

The presenter in an inspection meeting is ideally not the producer or author of the document being inspected. Not only does this oblige someone other than the author to look at the product thoroughly, but the meeting audience gets presented with a potentially different interpretation of the material. The other people in the meeting are the inspectors, representing different viewpoints.

Testers participating in any kind of review see the product differently than developers: "How is this thing going to work? If I test it this way, what's going to happen?" As testers we are working out what problems we're going to find when we test it. Our attention is drawn to weak areas of which we might not otherwise have been aware. That is why it is so important that testers are part of the inspection or review process – they bring a unique viewpoint to the meeting.

Any work product that's important can and should be inspected – a project plan, an engineering drawing, a user manual, a test plan. Appendix B includes a generic checklist for use on any document.

Walkthroughs

Walkthroughs are less formal than inspections mainly because of the lack of preparation. In walkthroughs the participants simply come to the meeting; the presenter prepares (usually the author of the product), and there's no additional effort by the participants prior to the meeting.

Walkthroughs: key elements

Objective:
- to detect defects and to become familiar with the material.

Elements:
- a planned meeting where only the presenter must prepare;
- a team of 2–7 people, led by the producer/author;
- the presenter is usually the producer.

Input:
- element under examination, objectives for the walkthrough, applicable standards.

Output:
- report.

Walkthroughs can cover more material than inspections and reviews because the presenter is the producer, and the other participants do not have a heavy participating work load. They therefore provide an opportunity for larger numbers of people to become familiar with the material.

Occasionally, walkthroughs are used for purposes of communication rather than for discovering defects. Software may be "inherited." We don't know exactly what's there so we organize a walkthrough to go through it, page by page, with the key people in the room. If defects are found, that's fine, but the main goal is to familiarize ourselves with the product.

The disadvantage of walkthroughs is that a review tends to be less objective when the presenter is the producer.

From the point of view of finding defects, preparation by participants in inspections and formal reviews usually raise more penetrating issues.

Buddy checks

Any form of human testing, even undisciplined testing, is better than none, provided it is performed by someone other than the author and its objective is to detect defects. There may, for instance, be occasions when it is inappropriate or impossible to get material inspected or formally reviewed.

However, simply giving a document to someone else and asking them to look at it closely will turn up defects we might never find on our own. Some studies show that such desk reviews can be extremely efficient, and they can be a good training ground for finding errors in the product, not the person.

Getting leverage on verification

What (and how much) verification to do?

We have to ask ourselves:

- How many defects are we finding as a result of these reviews?
- How many defects are getting through reviews and getting found in later validation testing?
- What percentage of them are left at the end of testing and only being found by customers?

Verification activities are implemented in an order where the size of the work product, its level of detail, and the cost to verify it are increasing, while the potential payoff is decreasing. This means that, if resources or schedule limitations preclude any of the verification activities (and they almost always will), candidates for elimination should be considered in the reverse order of their occurrence.

Requirements verification offers the biggest potential saving to software development efforts. It can detect many deficiencies that can otherwise go undetected until late in the development cycle, where correction is much more expensive because problems have migrated to other phases. Furthermore, the requirements stage is often where more than 50% of the defects are actually introduced.

In general, formal reviews and inspections are recommended. They are more expensive in the short term, but if done properly, the benefits will always outweigh the costs. They will detect a significant percentage of the errors, and the inherent data collection method is a useful metric for development performance. The success of these methods, and their cost effectiveness, can be measured.

Because they are time consuming and require intense concentration, inspections typically deal with relatively low volumes of material. Like all testing activities, verification of large work products will not be exhaustive and will usually involve risk assessments and trade-offs.

It can be a good idea to "mix and match" verification methods. There are times when it is appropriate to say: "This is the part of the code that's critical to us; it's the heart of the system, so we'll do a proper inspection on it. We're going to get several carefully chosen people and go through every line of the specification." Sampling of important documents can also be useful. Inspecting samples can provide a good estimate of the quality of the document and the number of errors in the uninspected parts of it.

On the other hand we may say: "Here's another part of the code that's not so important. It is not the heart of the system, and we don't want to invest in an inspection." In this case, we may want to do a less formal review or desk check or an informal walkthrough or variations on these. There are always trade-offs, and this is where risk analysis comes into play (see Chapter 5).

Verification is almost always more effective overall than validation testing. It may find defects that are nearly impossible to detect during validation testing. Most importantly, it allows us to find and detect the defects at the earliest possible time.

In most organizations the distribution of verification/validation defects is 20/80, or even less for verification. As a general strategy, we should be working toward a higher proportion of verification, though this can entail a major cultural change. Try verification in one new area, one that shows results fairly quickly and easily, to get people's support and enthusiasm. Then do a little bit more, slowly shifting the percentages.

Checklists: *the* verification tool

An important tool for verification, especially in more formal forms of verification like inspections, is the checklist. There are generic checklists that can be applied at a high level and maintained for each type of inspection. In other words, there is a checklist for requirements, a checklist for functional design specifications, a checklist for internal design specifications, a checklist for test plans. We can develop our own checklists for anything that we may want to review.

> **Sample generic checklists**
>
> The following checklists are included in Appendix B:
> - Requirements verification checklist
> - Functional design verification checklist
> - Internal design verification checklist
> - Generic code verification checklist (1)
> - Generic code verification checklist (2)
> - Code verification checklist for "C"
> - Code verification checklist for "COBOL"
> - Generic document verification checklist

Development and testing often have different checklists. Testing checklists tend to be orientated towards reliability and usability of the product. Development checklists are usually more focused on maintainability and things like guidelines for coding standards.

What is important is to make use of and build on generic checklists, but also to develop our own checklists within our organization for specific purposes and specific projects. These checklists should reflect our chosen focus and our particular present level of maturity in verification testing.

Checklists are an important part of testware. To get maximum leverage on verification, they should be carefully kept, improved, developed, updated – and someone has to take responsibility for this. They are a vital tool for verification testing; they are an important training device; they ensure continuity of the verification effort through different projects and different personnel, and they provide a record of the organization's progress in verification.

Verifying documents at different phases

Verifying requirements

The purpose of the requirements phase is to ensure that the users' needs are properly understood before translating them into design. Requirements are difficult to develop because it is hard to distinguish needs from wants. They will usually change in later phases and have always been the weakest link in the software chain. What do we mean by requirements and what kind of questions are we asking when we do requirements verification?

What's the capability that's needed by the user? What are we trying to provide for the customer? What do they want? The answer is a statement of requirement. The IEEE/ANSI definition is:

> *A requirement is a condition of capability needed by a user to solve a problem or achieve an objective.*

> *A requirement is a condition of capability that must be met by or possessed by a system or system component to satisfy a contract, standard, specification, or other formally imposed documents.*

Requirements may be expressed in formally composed documents or in an informal communication that defines the users' needs. They may be explicit, or implicit, but they are always there, and the purpose of this phase of our testing effort is to ensure that the users' needs are properly understood before we go any further.

One difficulty is to keep requirements strictly separate from solutions to those requirements. These two are frequently confused in documents produced at the early stages of the development process. The other difficulty is to realize that, even in the best of worlds, the requirements are going to change.

In the early days as testers we used to say, "We have to freeze the requirements. We have to get agreement that the requirements will never change, and then make sure that they never do." However, this is unrealistic because in real-world projects requirements do change. What we have to learn is to handle and control the change through proper verification of requirements and configuration management of the various versions (see Chapter 6) and provide ourselves with a solid framework for later testing.

The properties of good requirements specifications

The following are the properties that all good requirements specifications should have:

- visible
- clear (unambiguous)
- complete
- consistent (conflicting requirements must be prioritized)
- reasonable (achievable)
- measurable (quantifiable, testable)
- modifiable
- traceable
- dependent requirements identified.

The IEEE/ANSI guide to software requirements specifications is a very useful reference. It helps customers identify what they want; it helps suppliers understand what they have to provide, and it helps individuals involved with requirements to understand what they're trying to accomplish.

Help from IEEE/ANSI

IEEE/ANSI Standard 830-1993, Recommended Practice for Software Requirements Specifications, helps:

- software customers to accurately describe what they wish to obtain;
- software suppliers to understand exactly what the customer wants;
- individuals to accomplish the following goals:
  - develop standard software requirements specifications outline for their own organizations;
  - define the form and content of their specific software requirements specifications;
  - develop additional local supporting items such as requirements quality checklists or a requirements writers' handbook.

Frequently, the quality of a requirements document is a function of the producer, their skills, whether they know how to write requirements, and whether they are familiar with the standards. The quality of requirements is an important indicator of the level of maturity of an organization. If there is no life cycle, if there is no agreement that there will be a requirements document and there's no agreement on who writes it, what should be in it, or even what are the frameworks for acceptable requirements, development will be difficult and proper testing will be extremely difficult.

When we review requirements, we should be looking for basic functionality, but we need more than that. We may, for instance, need some definitions. Requirements frequently contain important terms and everybody assumes that we know what they mean.

Requirements checklist – sample items

The following is an extract from a generic requirements verification checklist:

- *Precise, unambiguous, and clear*
  Each item is exact and not vague; there is a single interpretation; the meaning of each item is understood; the specification is easy to read.

- *Consistent*
  No item conflicts with another item in the specification.

- *Relevant*
  Each item is pertinent to the problem and its eventual solution.

- *Testable*
  During program development and acceptance testing, it will be possible to determine whether the item has been satisfied.

- *Traceable*
  During program development and testing, it will be possible to trace each item through the various stages of development.

A more complete requirements verification checklist is in Appendix B.

Requirements may make frequent reference to vital, essential issues like security, usability, maintainability, and performance that are entirely non-specific or unexplained. When we're reading requirements from a testability standpoint all this vagueness is revealed for what it is. It's hard to test what constitutes "very good performance." What we can do is come back and say, "Well what did you mean by 'very good'; is that two seconds response time; does it mean 24 hours – or what?" The concept of testability is closely linked to the concept of measurability. Generally, the more quantifiable the requirements, the simpler it is to derive tests for the success of the system that results from them. Testers can provide requirements writers with the framework for the kinds of items that need to be there, like performance specifications, or usability metrics, or maintainability standards.

The testers' viewpoint on requirements is to look for anything that can be a problem. Is it unambiguous, complete, consistent, reasonable? Does it seem achievable? Is it traceable? Is it measurable from a testing standpoint? Verifying requirements provides fertile ground for development improvements as well as later testing. Asking "how can I test this?" will often produce better solutions from product designers as well as ideas about what and how to test.

Exercise on requirements verification

- Demonstrate the effectiveness of requirements verification by trying it out on the requirements document in Appendix C, a simple requirements specification for a reservation system. It can be verified with anything from a one-man "buddy check" to a full-scale inspection. Remember that successful verification takes time.

- Use the requirements verification checklist in Appendix B. Add to the checklist any new items that should be checked in future documents on the basis of this particular verification.

- Record the time taken to do the exercise.

- Estimate the time/cost consequences if the errors found had been allowed to migrate to later stages of development, or even to the user.

Solution: The consolidated notes on this document follows the exercise. It represents four groups of testing practitioners reviewing this document for approximately 30 minutes.

The requirements have been inspected; the changes have been made; the defects have been handled; the requirements have been signed off as approved by the review group. We now have a good basis for test design, for change negotiations and for validation. As a result of participating in requirements verification, we have already learned something about the product and can now plan for validation testing and how it's going to work. We're already ahead of the game!

Verifying the functional design

Functional design is the process of translating user requirements into the set of external (human) interfaces. The output of the process is the functional design specification, which describes the product's behavior as seen by an observer external to the product. It should describe everything the user can see and should avoid describing what the user cannot see. It is eventually translated into an internal design as well as user manuals. It should not include internal information, internal data structures, data diagrams or flow diagrams; they belong in the internal design specification which is the next step in the process.

How is verifying functional design different than verifying the requirements? If requirements are the most important, functional design is the next most important, simply because it is early in the process.

Functional design checklist – sample items

The following is an extract from a generic functional design verification checklist:

- When a term is defined explicitly somewhere, try substituting that definition in place of the term.
- When a structure is described in words, try to sketch a picture of the structure being described.
- When a calculation is specified, work at least two examples by hand and give them as examples in the specification.
- When searching behind certainty statements, *push the search back* as many levels as are needed to achieve the kind of certainty a computer will need.
- Watch for *vague* words, such as *some, sometimes, often, usually, ordinarily, customarily, most,* or *mostly*.

A more complete functional design verification checklist is in Appendix B.

The goal in verifying a functional design is to determine how successfully the user requirements have been incorporated into the functional design. The concept of traceability starts to operate here. We have requirements and we use the requirements document again at this stage as a source document for verifying the functional design. Every paragraph in the requirements should be reflected in the functional design specifications. If it's not, maybe it was dropped completely (but where is this recorded?) or maybe someone simply forgot to implement it.

One of the most common failings of the functional design specifications is incompleteness. Good inspectors or reviewers don't just read what's in front of them. We have to constantly ask: "What's missing?" and keep asking ourselves what should have been written on the page. Try to imagine, if you had been writing the document, what you would have included before you read the section. How should this be described functionally? How should it look to the end user? Pretending to be the designer writing the document enables you to see some of the errors of omission. These are the most important errors to find.

The requirements document itself often has a number of sources, such as standards, correspondence, minutes of meetings, etc. If so, that's where traceability starts. It is also important to look out for unwarranted additions.

Exercise on verifying functional design specification

- Demonstrate the effectiveness of functional design verification by trying it out on the functional design document in Appendix C, a functional design specification for a sales system.
- Use the functional design verification checklist in Appendix B.

Solution: The consolidated notes on this document follows the exercise. It represents four groups of testing practitioners reviewing this document for approximately 30 minutes.

Verifying the internal design

Internal design is the process of translating the functional specification into a detailed set of data structures, data flows, and algorithms. The output of the process is the internal design specification which shows how the product is to be built. Multiple internal design specifications, representing successive levels of abstraction, may be produced. If possible, each of them should be verified.

Internal design checklist – sample items

The following is an extract from a typical internal design verification checklist:

- Does the design document contain a description of the procedure that was used to do preliminary design or is there a reference to such a procedure?
- Is there a model of the user interface to the computing system?
- Is there a high-level functional model of the proposed computing system?
- Are the major implementation alternatives and their evaluations represented in the document?

A more complete internal design verification checklist is in Appendix B.

There is a recommended practice for software design descriptions from IEEE/ANSI in the software engineering standards documentation. It has recommendations for locating information, formats, and ways of organizing the material.

Help from IEEE/ANSI

IEEE/ANSI Standard 1016-1987, IEEE Recommended Practice for Software Design Descriptions (Reaff. 1993), specifies the necessary information content and recommends an organization for software design descriptions. See Appendix A.

Internal design specifications are invaluable to have as a testing perspective. Seeing how the product is going to be built and thinking how the whole system is going to come together enables testers to design additional internals-based tests.

Reviewing internal design involves using checklists, tracing the path back to functional design and back to requirements, and trying to see whether we agree with the algorithms and how they're being put together. We're searching for defects, but we're also thinking, "How would we test that?"

For example, if there's a table that's used in part of the internal design, testers can start asking some questions which are pertinent for testing: "How big is the table? Why are there 25 entries? How do we fill that table? How do we overflow that table? What happens if nothing goes in that table?"

Such questions will provoke good testing ideas. As soon as we start to look at a description of an internal document, the limits within the product become clearer. It shows up boundary conditions; it will warn us about performance and possible failure conditions and all kinds of other internal considerations. From a testing standpoint, whether there are formal internal design specifications or whether we do reviews of them, we can learn a lot about the product by getting this information and thinking about it from a testing perspective.

Verifying the code

Coding is the process of translating the detailed design specification into a specific set of code. The output of the process is the source code itself. This is often the place where companies start when they begin doing walkthroughs and inspections. Sometimes it is the most comfortable place to commence, which is all right as long as we realize it's not the most efficient place to be. Once people are doing walkthroughs and inspections on code, and getting comfortable with the process and learning how to exploit it, we can move them toward reviewing the documents that exist long before there is any code. After all, if we're coding to a poor specification and to the wrong requirements, we've already wasted a lot of time!

Verifying the code involves the following activities:

(1) Comparing the code with internal design specifications.
(2) Examining the code against a language-specific checklist.
(3) Using a static analysis tool to check for compliance with the syntactic/content requirements.
(4) Verifying the correspondence of terms in code with data dictionary and with internal design specification.
(5) Searching for new boundary conditions, possible performance bottlenecks, and other internal considerations which may form the basis for additional validation tests.

companies do a formal code review. Participants are given the code in
⬛ce; they read through it, look for defects, come to a meeting, walk the
⬛tep by step and testers are there helping to find defects and asking for
⬛ation. On the other hand it can be very informal. It can simply be a
⬛ check, where one person just looks at another person's code and marks
⬛ors in it. On a small scale it can work very effectively.

---

checklist – sample items

The following are typical headings with a single example under each from a
generic code verification checklist:

Data reference errors
Is an unset or unitialized variable referenced?

Data declaration errors
Are there variables with similar names?

Computation errors
Is the target variable of an assignment smaller than the right-hand expression?

Comparison errors
Are the conversion rules for comparisons between data or variables of
inconsistent type or length handled?

Control flow errors
Is there a possibility of premature loop exit?

Interface errors
If the module has multiple entry points, is a parameter ever referenced that is
not associated with the current point of entry?

Input/output errors
Are there grammatical errors in program output text?

Portability
How is the data organized (e.g., packed structures)?

Complete generic and particular code verification checklists are in Appendix B.

We should always be thinking from a testing perspective. Whenever we
look at a piece of code, we will think of new tests that we could not have
thought of by only reading the requirement or the functional design specification. Often we can spot the error conditions that will provoke failure when
the code is first executed. Frequently, developers do straight line checking
which does not find these kinds of errors. They will give the code to testing,
but the first time the path is executed the whole system crashes.

If code verification is being done more formally, existing checklists in the
organization can be used, or a generic checklist can be used as a starting point
(see Appendix B) for building a customized version.

Getting the best from verification

The author

People who have their work reviewed in public see themselves in a hot seat, and naturally tend to get defensive. It's important to work hard and consistently for the team spirit attitude: "We are here to find defects in our work products, not to attack individuals for the failures in their part of it." As authors, we should be aware that we are in a position that we may find hard to handle at first, but we have everything to gain from having our work reviewed in this way. Next time around when we're on the team, we should remember to treat the author as we would like to be treated when our work is being reviewed.

As a member of the inspection team, avoid discussions of style. We are there to evaluate the product, not its producer. It's tempting to get diverted into "I would have said it this way," or "It would be much better if you wrote it this way instead of that way." Style issues are not about the content of the information, but the way it has been written. There may, however, be legitimate issues of clarity or definition of terms which ultimately affect the content.

Whatever level of formality is being used in verification, be tactful, be reasonable, and be sensitive to other people's egos. Do any preparation required for inspections properly, and at the inspection meeting, raise issues – don't try to solve them.

If we can develop these attitudes successfully within the testing organization (and acting as an example goes a very long way), we will be the instigators of a critical culture change.

The development team

Reviews and inspections can help with communication and with motivation, sometimes through a sense of pride or even embarrassment. If people know their work product is going to be inspected they tend to do a better job.

Feedback can be very positive. There are times in review meetings when producers/authors get a sense of "that looks good, that's a good way to do it" from the team, and it becomes, without being formally adopted, common good practice within the organization. Feedback sharpens people's level of performance in a constructive way, and in six months to a year, we'll get a reduction in defects, just because we know our material is going to be under scrutiny the next time there is a review.

The other issue that is really important is communication. We don't measure our success in inspection purely by defects that are being found. Inspection is also about improving the software development process. One of the things that contributes to the value of the inspection is that people start communicating about things that they need to know to do their jobs properly.

For example, being on an inspection team enables testers to find out basic information about the product that they didn't have before. This communication value of inspection should never be ignored.

Verification, especially at the early stages, can help with communication not only within the development environment, but throughout the organization. If we are doing requirements verification, for instance, ideally we need the marketing people, as well as the test people and development people there, and maybe support people as well. It's a golden opportunity to spread understanding and better communication to a wider group.

The inspection team

Inspection is difficult because there is no detailed cookbook method for any given type of work product. Each type of work product requires different expertise and thought processes. Critical thinking, which must often transcend even the most robust and well-defined inspection checklists, is required.

Inspection also requires intense concentration and is very fatiguing if overused. It requires the ability to detect omissions. Most people react only to what they see in front of them. The best reviewers and inspectors must ask "What's missing?" or "What should be written here that isn't?" The tough thing is to ask what should have been on the page but isn't there. Good reviewers, especially good inspection team people, are worth their weight in gold in organizations. After a while, everybody knows who they are, and they are constantly in demand for any kind of verification activity.

Cost-effective verification

Verification is just as productive and important as validation testing, if not more so. It has the potential to detect defects at the earliest possible stage, thereby minimizing the cost of correction. But is the verification process itself cost effective? Do we save more than we spend by finding errors early? The short answer is that it has been demonstrated again and again that verification, although it isn't free, is cost effective.

We should therefore try to verify critical documents, or at least some parts of them. On a large work product, we will almost certainly feel we can't do all the ideal complete code reviews and formal specification and design reviews. We may want to use walkthroughs for some parts, instead of having formal reviews, and we may want to do desk checks for some items. These are all decisions based on the particular case.

We can increase the cost effectiveness of verification by having a good configuration management system (see Chapter 6). Somebody must make sure we're not verifying the wrong thing at the wrong time, and that what we verify is the same thing that we validation-test and that we eventually ship.

Three critical success factors for implementing verification

Success factor 1: process ownership

If we are not already using verification or we need to improve the way we are doing it, the process needs a champion. The champion can be anybody who really is interested in it, who cares a lot about it, and who will take ownership for the process and will make it happen. It could be someone in the development organization, who knows inspections are a good thing. It could be a quality assurance person; it could be a process expert, or someone in the process engineering group. It could be a full-time job or it could be a part-time job. When companies get really big they hire people to do nothing but organize formal verification processes. In smaller companies this is neither necessary nor possible. The important thing is that somebody must become the champion of the method and work in the medium and long term to gradually gain support for it.

Success factor 2: management support

Frequently, it is management that initiates the adoption of inspections. Whether or not they are initiating the process, it is important that managers are well briefed on inspections and their benefits. It is unreasonable to expect them to spend resources and support the effort if they don't see the long-term gains. It can be difficult for anyone with different pressures and different immediate problems to solve to understand why it's worth putting resources into these early testing efforts.

You should promote support for inspections by getting out early results. If possible, collect data on the errors found by verifying at the early stages and compare this to the estimated costs if they had been allowed to migrate to the later stages. Get people who aren't so enthusiastic about these methods to a meeting to discuss problems with a particular work product, and then demonstrate with a small, live inspection how effective inspections are in their own organization and on their own material. Show them it's possible to monitor the cost effectiveness of the new process.

Success factor 3: training

Training in reviews and inspections is crucial, including specific training for practitioners on how to perform reviews and inspections, including costs, benefits, and dealing with the human and cultural issues. Training should also include performing inspections in a workshop setting of real work products from the local environment. Everyone who is going to be inspecting documents should be trained. Where this is not possible, an experienced team with a good grasp of the human issues involved can absorb a new member.

Help from SIRO

Software Inspection and Review Organization (SIRO)

This organization was formed to exchange new ideas and information about group-based software examinations. It facilitates emerging inspection and review techniques, provides a clearing house for resources, and surveys/reports on the current use of inspections and reviews.

Contact:
SIRO
PO Box 61015
Sunnyvale, CA 94088-1015

Recommendations

Inspections are recommended first and foremost because they have proven to be the most effective, most practical method of verification. Inspections are probably the oldest methodology in the history of software development. They have been used successfully for at least 25 years. So while inspection techniques have evolved over this time, you won't be suggesting untried leading edge methods when you suggest implementing inspections in your organization. They work. Getting the right people in a room to look at the right material in a systematic, objective way is simply common sense and good basic communication.

There's a real trade-off between verification and validation testing. In doing verification we begin to ease the pain in validation testing. Most testing organizations experience "The Chaos Zone" when they only do functional testing or system testing. At that point, all of the code, of which testing has little or no prior knowledge, is thrown into the testing department. All kinds of defects are found through hasty testing in unfamiliar territory. Shipment dates are missed and pressure is created because testers are operating in an unfamiliar environment where there should be an opportunity to get acquainted with the product and find many defects a lot earlier.

Get started by inspecting some key material. Typically, an organization will have all kinds of projects all at different stages. Some projects may be so far along that it doesn't make sense to implement verification on them.

It is usually better not to go for a "big bang" approach and implement formal inspections on all documentation from a certain point in time. It's best to pick some high-risk material with a high pay-off on a number of different projects first. Perhaps start by reviewing all new requirement specifications or all new and changed code on critical projects. Build support while measuring and tracking enthusiasm from peers. Then do inspections on a wider range of documentation and demonstrate the results.

Show management or colleagues who don't know about inspections the results of the requirements and functional design verification exercises in this chapter. Be sure to include the time resources used and the estimated consequences of allowing the errors found to migrate to later stages.

References

Bender, D. (1993). "Writing testable requirements," *Software Testing Analysis & Review (STAR) Conference Proceedings*. (This provides a set of practical guidelines for writing testable requirements.)

Fagan, M.E. (1976). "Design and code inspection to reduce errors in program development," *IBM Systems Journal*, **15**(3).

Freedman, D.P. and Weinberg, G.M. (1990). *Handbook of Walkthroughs, Inspections, and Technical Reviews*. New York: Dorset.

Gilb, T. and Graham, D. (1993). *Software Inspection*. Wokingham: Addison-Wesley.

IEEE/ANSI (1988). IEEE Standard for Software Reviews and Audits, IEEE Std 1028-1988.

Chapter 8
Validation testing

Validation overview

Let us begin with eight axioms that apply to all validation testing:

(1) Testing can be used to show the presence of errors, but never their absence.

(2) One of the most difficult problems in testing is knowing when to stop.

(3) Avoid unplanned, non-reusable, throw-away test cases unless the program is truly a throw-away program.

(4) A necessary part of a test case is a definition of the expected output or result. Always carefully compare the actual versus the expected results of each test.

(5) Test cases must be written for invalid and unexpected, as well as valid and expected, input conditions. "Invalid" is defined as a condition that is outside the set of valid conditions and should be diagnosed as such by the program being tested.

(6) Test cases must be written to generate desired output conditions. Less experienced testers tend to think only from the input perspective. Experienced testers determine the inputs required to generate a pre-designed set of outputs.

(7) With the exception of unit and integration testing, a program should not be tested by the person or organization that developed it. Practical cost considerations usually require developers do unit and integration testing.

(8) The number of undiscovered errors is directly proportional to the number of errors already discovered.

The IEEE/ANSI definition is as follows:

> *Validation* is the process of evaluating a system or component during or at the end of the development process to determine whether it satisfies specified requirements.

The eight axioms are quite useful, but how do we determine in practice whether a program does in fact meet its requirements? There are two keys:

(1) Developing tests that will determine whether the product satisfies the users' requirements, as stated in the requirements specification.
(2) Developing tests that will determine whether the product's actual behavior matches the desired behavior, as described in the functional design specification.

Even though the internal design and code are derived from the functional design, it is usually not necessary to understand either of them to determine whether the end product meets its requirements.

In IEEE/ANSI usage, note the word "requirements" includes both user requirements and functional interfaces. In practice, these should be created and maintained as two distinct documents. The high-level requirements are written from a customer or market perspective, while the functional specification is written from an engineering perspective. A significant issue in many companies is trying to define a clear boundary between marketing and engineering specification responsibilities. By defining the format and content of these two key documents separately, many organizations manage to obtain agreement on organizational ownership; e.g., marketing is responsible for creating the requirements specification, and software engineering is responsible for the functional design specification (see Figure 8.1).

Coverage

How do we measure how thoroughly tested a product is? What is the measure of "testedness"? To what degree do our test cases adequately cover the product? How do we quantitatively measure how good a job we are doing as testers?

The execution of a given test case against program P will:

- address (cover) certain requirements of P;
- utilize (cover) certain parts of P's functionality;
- exercise (cover) certain parts of P's internal logic.

We have to be sure we have enough tests at each of these levels.

The measures of testedness for P are the degrees to which the collective set of test cases for P enhance the requirements coverage, the function coverage and the logic coverage.

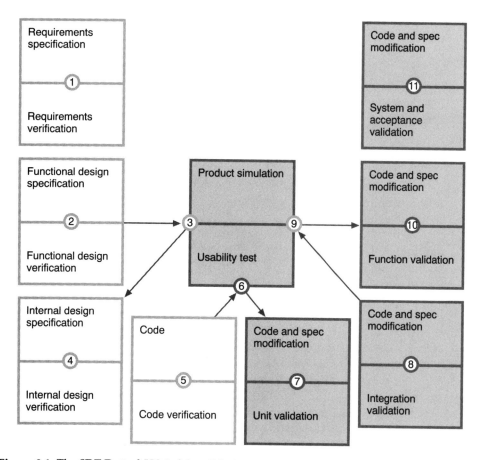

Figure 8.1 The SDT Dotted-U Model, validation. (© 1993, 1994 Software Development Technologies)

Fundamental testing strategies

Black-box testing and white-box testing are the two fundamental testing strategies. They are strategies, not technical or analytical methods.

Black-box tests are derived from the functional design specification, without regard to the internal program structure. Black-box testing tests the product against the end user, external specifications. Black-box testing is done without any internal knowledge of the product. It is important in practice to try to test, or at least write, detailed test plans for requirements and functional specifications tests without too much knowledge of the code. Understanding the code changes the way the requirements are seen, and test design should not be "contaminated" by this knowledge too early.

Black-box testing will not test hidden functions (i.e., functions implemented but not described in the functional design specification), and the errors associated with them will not be found in black-box testing.

White-box tests require knowledge of the internal program structure and are derived from the internal design specification or the code. They will not detect missing functions (i.e., those described in the functional design specification but not supported by the internal specification or code).

Validation mission vs. test coverage

Exhaustive testing is impossible and the testing of any program will be necessarily incomplete. The negative effects of this incompleteness are minimized by identifying the subset of all possible test cases that has the highest probability of detecting the most errors. In this way we can find the greatest possible number of errors with a finite number of tests.

Test coverage has three components: requirements coverage, function coverage, and logic coverage. IEEE/ANSI clearly states the importance of the first two of these, but in fact logic coverage is also very important for two reasons:

(1) it indirectly improves function coverage;
(2) it is necessary for the testing of logic paths that are not discernible from the external functionality (e.g., a math function that uses completely different algorithms, depending on the values of the input arguments).

Coverage is typically referred to at the statement level. The simplest form is the percentage of the statements in the program that are being executed by the test: "80% coverage" means that 80% of the statements in the program have been tested. On a project involving compiler testing, the author discovered that, if by going to 75% coverage, we found x bugs, then by increasing coverage from 75% to 85%, another x bugs will be found. Likewise from 85 to 90% we find two to three times x bugs again! Generally stated, the probability of finding new defects is inversely proportional to the amount of code not yet covered. The closer we are to achieving 100% coverage, the more likely it becomes that we are searching in previously un-navigated territory and the more likely it is that we will find more defects per line of code.

Test basis

The basis of a test is the source material (of the product under test) that provides the stimulus for the test. In other words, it is the area targeted as the potential source of an error:

- Requirements-based tests are based on the requirements document.
- Function-based tests are based on the functional design specification.
- Internals-based tests are based on the internal design specification or code.

Function-based and internals-based tests will fail to detect situations where requirements are not met. Internals-based tests will fail to detect errors in functionality.

Validation strategies

Given the alternatives of black-box and white-box testing, and the need for requirements, function, and logic test coverage, what should our overall strategy be?

- *Requirements-based tests* should employ the black-box strategy. User requirements can be tested without knowledge of the internal design specification or the code. Tests are based on the requirements document but formulated by using the functional design specification.
- *Function-based tests* should employ the black-box strategy. Using the functional design specification to design function-based tests is both necessary and sufficient. The requirements and internal design specifications are unnecessary for function-based tests.
- *Internals-based tests* must necessarily employ the white-box strategy. Tests can be formulated by using the functional design specification.

There are two basic requirements which apply to all validation tests:

(1) definition of results
(2) repeatability.

A necessary part of a test case is a definition of the expected output or result. If the expected result is not pre-defined, it is all too easy to interpret the actual result as correct. Once again, it was Myers who saw the significance of our perceptual and cognitive mechanisms for testing: "The eye sees what it wants to see." (Myers, 1979: p. 12)

The test case should be repeatable. In other words, it should produce identical results each time it is run against the same software/hardware configuration. When actual and expected results disagree, the failure should be able to be recreated by development in its debugging efforts. However, repeatability is not always possible, for example, when the software and/or hardware is handling asynchronous processes. Here are some IEEE/ANSI definitions:

A *test*:
(i)   An activity in which a system or component is executed under specified conditions, the results are observed or recorded, and an evaluation is made of some aspect of the system or component.
(ii) A set of one or more test cases.

IEEE/ANSI's second definition of "test" requires additional terms to identify separate and distinct, lower-level tests within a single test case.

A *test case*:
(i)   A set of test inputs, execution conditions, and expected results developed for a particular objective.
(ii) The smallest entity that is always executed as a unit, from beginning to end.

A test case may perform any number of discrete *subtests*.

A *test procedure*:
(i)   The detailed instructions for the set-up, execution, and evaluation of results for a given test case.
(ii) A test case may be used in more than one test procedure. (See Figure 8.2.)

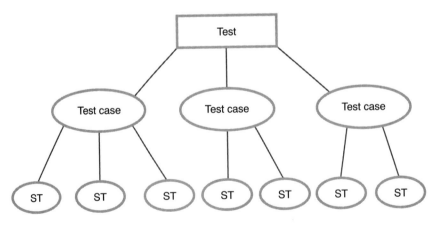

ST = Subtest

Figure 8.2 Tests, test cases, and subtests. (© 1993, 1994 Software Development Technologies)

Validation methods

Proven test-design methods provide a more intelligent and effective means of identifying tests than a purely random approach.

This section describes some detailed technical and analytical methods for designing high-yield tests. Each method is described in testing literature. The ones outlined here are the most commonly used, practical, and useful. Each has strengths and weaknesses (i.e., types of errors it is likely to detect and those it will fail to detect).

Black-box methods for function-based tests

The following methods are commonly used:

- equivalence partitioning
- boundary-value analysis
- error guessing.

The following are lesser-used methods:

- cause-effect graphing
- syntax testing
- state transition testing
- graph matrix.

Equivalence partitioning

Equivalence partitioning is a systematic process that identifies, on the basis of whatever information is available, a set of interesting classes of input conditions to be tested, where each class is representative of (or covers) a large set of other possible tests. If partitioning is applied to the product under test, the product is going to behave in much the same way for all members of the class.

The aim is to minimize the number of test cases required to cover these input conditions.

There are two distinct steps. The first is to identify the equivalence classes (ECs) and the second is to identify the test cases.

(1) *Identifying equivalence classes*
   For each external input:
   (i)   If the input specifies *a range* of valid values, define one valid EC (within the range) and two invalid ECs (one outside each end of the range).

Example: If the input requires a month in the range of 1–12, define one valid EC for months 1 though 12 and two invalid ECs (month<1 and month>12).

(ii) If the input specifies the *number* (N) of valid values, define one valid EC and two invalid ECs (none, and more than N).

Example: If the input requires the titles of at least three but no more than eight books, then define one valid EC and two invalid ECs (<3 and >8 books).

(iii) If the input specifies a *set* of valid values, define one valid EC (within the set) and one invalid EC (outside the set).

Example: If the input requires one of the names TOM, DICK, or HARRY, then define one valid EC (using one of the valid names) and one invalid EC (using the name JOE).

(iv) If there is reason to believe that the program handles each valid input differently, then define one valid EC per valid input.

(v) If the input specifies a "must be" situation, define one valid EC and one invalid EC.

Example: If the first character of the input must be numeric, then define one valid EC where the first character is a number and one invalid EC where the first character is not a number.

(vi) If there is reason to believe that elements in an EC are not handled in an identical manner by the program, subdivide the EC into smaller ECs.

(2) *Identifying test cases*

(i)   Assign a unique number to each EC.

(ii) Until all valid ECs have been covered by test cases, write a new test case covering as many of the uncovered ECs as possible.

(iii) Until all invalid ECs have been covered by test cases, write a test case that covers one, and only one, of the uncovered invalid ECs.

(iv) If multiple invalid ECs are tested in the same test case, some of those tests may never be executed because the first test may mask other tests or terminate execution of the test case.

Reminder: A necessary part of any test case is a description of the expected results, even for tests that use invalid inputs.

Equivalence partitioning significantly reduces the number of input conditions to be tested by identifying classes of conditions that are equivalent to many other conditions. It does not test combinations of input conditions.

Exercise on equivalence partitioning

Equivalence partitioning looks easy, but takes practice. For practice we have included an exercise along with one possible solution. Read the program description below, and then complete the worksheet that follows.

FUNCTIONAL DESIGN SPECIFICATION FOR GOLFSCORE

GOLFSCORE is a program which calculates the scores of the participants in a golf tournament which is based on the following assumptions and scoring rules:

Assumptions:
(1) The number of courses played can be from 1 to 8.
(2) The number of participating golfers can be from 2 to 400.
(3) Each golfer plays each course once.
(4) A golfer's tournament score is the sum of his/her scores on each course.
(5) Each golf course has 18 holes, and par for each hole is 3, 4, or 5.

Scoring rules for each hole:

Strokes	Score
over par	0
par	1
1 under par	2
2 under par	4
>2 under par	6

Input
Input to GOLFSCORE is a formatted text file containing the following records, in sequence:

(1) **Course records.** One record for each golf course. Each record contains the name of the course and the par for each of its 18 holes.

Column 1:	Blank
Columns 2–19:	Course name
Columns 21–38:	Par for holes 1–18 (par is an integer 3, 4, or 5)

(2) **Delimiter record.** Denotes the end of the course records.

Column 1:	Non-blank
Columns 2–60:	Blank

(3) **Golfer records.** One record per golfer per course (in any order). Each record contains the name of the golfer, the name of the course, and the actual number of strokes taken for each of the 18 holes.

Column 1:	Blank
Columns 2–19:	Course name
Columns 22–39:	Golfer name
Columns 41–58:	Number of strokes taken for holes 1–18 (per hole, number of strokes is a single, non-zero digit)

(4) **Delimiter record.** Denotes the end of the golfer records.

Column 1:	Non-blank
Columns 2–60:	Blank

Output

GOLFSCORE produces the following output reports, showing:

(1) The names of the golfers, their scores for each course, their total scores, and their final rank in the tournament, sorted in descending order of total score.

(2) The same as report (1), but sorted alphabetically by golfer name.

(3) Per course, the same as report (1), but sorted in descending order of score on that course.

Each report contains one output record per golfer.

Worksheet

External input condition	Valid equivalence classes	Invalid equivalence classes

There are many possible solutions to this exercise. One possible solution can be found in Appendix D.

Boundary-value analysis

Boundary-value analysis is a variant and refinement of equivalence partitioning, with two major differences:

First, rather than selecting any element in an equivalence class as being representative, elements are selected such that each edge of the EC is the subject of a test. Boundaries are always a good place to look for defects.

Second, rather than focusing exclusively on input conditions, output conditions are also explored by defining output ECs. What can be output? What are the classes of output? What should I create as an input to force a useful set of classes that represent the outputs that ought to be produced?

The guidelines for boundary-value analysis are:

- If an input specifies a range of valid values, write test cases for the ends of the range and invalid-input test cases for conditions just beyond the ends.

  Example: If the input requires a real number in the range 0.0 to 90.0 degrees, then write test cases for 0.0, 90.0, –0.001, and 90.001.

- If an input specifies a number of valid values, write test cases for the minimum and maximum number of values and one beneath and beyond these values.

  Example: If the input requires the titles of at least 3, but no more than 8, books, then write test cases for 2, 3, 8, and 9 books.

- Use the above guidelines for each output condition.

Boundary-value analysis is not as simple as it sounds, because boundary conditions may be subtle and difficult to identify. The method does not test combinations of input conditions.

Exercise on boundary-value analysis

Using the same functional design specification for GOLFSCORE described above, make a list of boundary values to be tested. Be sure to consider both input and output conditions. A possible solution can be found in Appendix D.

Error guessing

Error guessing is an *ad hoc* approach, based on intuition and experience, to identify tests that are considered likely to expose errors. The basic idea is to make a list of possible errors or error-prone situations and then develop tests based on the list. What are the most common error-prone situations we have seen before? Defects' histories are useful. There is a high probability that defects that have been there in the past are the kind that are going to be there in the future.

Some items to try are:

- empty or null lists/strings
- zero instances/occurrences
- blanks or null characters in strings
- negative numbers.

One of the studies done by Myers (1979) states that the probability of errors remaining in the program is proportional to the number of errors that have been found so far. This alone provides a rich source of focus for productive error guessing.

Cause-effect graphing

Cause-effect graphing is a systematic approach to selecting a high-yield set of test cases that explore combinations of input conditions. It is a rigorous method for transforming a natural-language specification into a formal-language specification, and exposes incompleteness and ambiguities in the specification.

Deriving cause-effect tests

Cause-effect tests are derived as follows:
- Decompose the specification into workable pieces.
- Identify causes and their effects.
- Create a (Boolean) cause-effect graph.
- Annotate the graph with constraints describing combinations of causes and/or effects that are impossible.
- Convert the graphs into a limited-entry decision table by methodically tracing state conditions in the graph. Each column in the table represents a test case.
- The columns in the decision table are converted into test cases.

Cause-effect graphing explores combinations of input conditions. It produces non-redundant, high-yield tests. It is useful in functional (external) specification verification, because it exposes errors in the specification. However, it is difficult and time-consuming to implement. It is a much more practical proposition when there is a tool to convert the graph into a decision table.

Syntax testing

Syntax testing is a systematic method of generating valid and invalid input data to a program. It is applicable to programs that have a hidden language that defines the data (e.g., the interactive commands to operating systems and subsystems). It is usually ineffective if the language is explicit and formally developed, as in compilers.

Syntax testing is basically a shotgun method that relies on creating many test cases, and is not useful for semantics testing (use function tests). The key to syntax testing is to learn how to recognize hidden languages.

The steps in syntax testing are:

- Identify the target language (explicit or implicit).
- Define the language syntax formally.

- Test the valid cases first by covering the definition graph.
- Design tests, level by level, top to bottom, making only one error at a time, one level at a time.
- Test the invalid cases.
- Automate the creation and execution of the tests.

State transition testing

State transition testing is an analytical method, using finite-state machines, to design tests for programs that have many similar, but slightly different, control functions. It is primarily a functional testing tool and also has a high pay-off in functional design verification.

Graph matrix

A graph matrix is a simpler representation of a graph to organize the data. With a graph represented as a square matrix each row represents a node in the graph (node = 1, ..., n). Each column represents a node in the graph (node = 1, ..., n) and M(I,J) defines the relationship (if any) between node I and node J. (It is usually a sparse matrix because there is often no relationship between certain nodes.)

A graph matrix is used for proving things about graphs and for developing algorithms.

White-box methods for internals-based tests

Once white-box testing is started, there are a number of techniques to ensure the internal parts of the system are being adequately tested and that there is sufficient logic coverage.

The execution of a given test case against program P will exercise (cover) certain parts of P's internal logic. A measure of testedness for P is the degree of logic coverage produced by the collective set of test cases for P. White-box testing methods are used to increase logic coverage.

There are four basic forms of logic coverage:

(1) statement coverage
(2) decision (branch) coverage
(3) condition coverage
(4) path coverage.

White-box methods defined and compared

Figure 8.3 illustrates white-box methods. For example, to perform condition coverage, tests covering characteristics 1 and 3 are required. Tests covering 2 and 4 are not required. To perform multiple condition coverage, tests covering characteristics 1 and 4 are required. Such tests will automatically cover characteristics 1 and 2.

		Statement coverage	Decision coverage	Condition coverage	Decision/ condition coverage	Multiple condition coverage
1	Each statement is executed at least once	Y	Y	Y	Y	Y
2	Each decision takes on all possible outcomes at least once	N	Y	N	Y	implicit
3	Each condition in a decision takes on all possible outcomes at least once	N	N	Y	Y	implicit
4	All possible combinations of condition outcomes in each decision occur at least once	N	N	N	N	Y

Figure 8.3 The white-box methods defined and compared. Each column in this figure represents a distinct method of white-box testing, and each row (1–4) defines a different test characteristic. For a given method (column), "Y" in a given row means that the test characteristic is required for the method. "N" signifies no requirement. "Implicit" means the test characteristic is achieved implicitly by other requirements of the method. (© 1993, 1994 Software Development Technologies)

Exhaustive path coverage is generally impractical. However, there are practical methods, based on the other three basic forms, which provide increasing degrees of logic coverage.

Example of white-box coverage
To clarify the difference between these coverage methods, consider the following Pascal procedure. The goal of the example is to list one possible set of tests (sets of input data) which satisfies the criteria for each of the white-box coverage methods.

The liability procedure:

```
procedure liability (age, sex, married, premium ) ;
begin
        premium := 500 ;
        if ( (age < 25) and (sex = male) and (not married) ) then premium :=
        premium + 1500 ;
        else ( if ( married or (sex = female) ) then
                        premium := premium – 200 ;
                if ( (age > 45) and (age < 65) ) then
                        premium := premium – 100 ; )
        end ;
```

The three input parameters are age (integer), sex (male or female), and married (true or false). Keep in mind the following:

- *Statement coverage*: Each statement is executed at least once.
- *Decision coverage*: Each statement is executed at least once; each decision takes on all possible outcomes at least once.
- *Condition coverage*: Each statement is executed at least once; each condition in a decision takes on all possible outcomes at least once.
- *Decision/condition coverage*: Each statement is executed at least once; each decision takes on all possible outcomes at least once; each condition in a decision takes on all possible outcomes at least once.
- *Multiple/condition coverage*: Each statement is executed at least once; all possible combinations of condition outcomes in each decision occur at least once.

A logic coverage methods solution for the liability (insurance) procedure follows. The following notation is used in each table shown below.

The first column of each row denotes the specific "IF" statement from the exercise program. For example, "IF-2" means the second IF statement in the sample program.

The last column indicates a test-case number in parentheses. For example, "(3)" indicates test-case number 3. Any information following the test-case number is the test data itself in abbreviated form. For example, "23 F T" means age = 23, sex = Female, and married = True.

An asterisk (*) in any box means "wild card" or "any valid input."

Statement coverage	Age	Sex	Married	Test case

There are only two statements in this program, and any combination of inputs will provide coverage for both statements.

Decision coverage	Age	Sex	Married	Test case
IF-1	< 25	Male	False	(1) 23 M F
IF-1	< 25	Female	False	(2) 23 F F
IF-2	*	Female	*	(2)
IF-2	>= 25	Male	False	(3) 50 M F
IF-3	<= 45	Female (n1)	*	(2)
IF-3	> 45, < 65	*	*	(3)

Note (n1): This input is not necessary for IF-3, but it is necessary to ensure that IF-1 is false [if age < 25 and married is false] so that the *else* clause of IF-1 (and hence IF-3) will be executed.

Condition coverage	Age	Sex	Married	Test case
IF-1	< 25	Female	False	(1) 23 F F
IF-1	>= 25	Male	True	(2) 30 M T
IF-2	*	Male	True	(2)
IF-2	*	Female	False	(1)
IF-3	<= 45	*	*	(1)
IF-3	> 45	*	*	(3) 70 F F
IF-3	< 65	*	*	(2)
IF-3	>= 65	*	*	(3)

Note: These test cases fail to execute the *then* clauses of IF-1 and IF-3 as well as the (empty) *else* clause of IF-2.

Decision/condition coverage	Age	Sex	Married	Test case
IF-1 (decision)	< 25	Male	False	(1) 23 M F
IF-1 (decision)	< 25	Female	False	(2) 23 F F
IF-1 (condition)	< 25	Female	False	(2)
IF-1 (condition)	>= 25	Male	True	(3) 70 M T
IF-2 (decision)	*	Female	*	(2)
IF-2 (decision)	>= 25	Male	False	(4) 50 M F
IF-2 (condition)	*	Male	True	(3)
IF-2 (condition)	*	Female	False	(2)
IF-3 (decision)	<= 45	*	*	(2)
IF-3 (decision)	> 45, < 65	*	*	(4)
IF-3 (condition)	<= 45	*	*	(2)
IF-3 (condition)	> 45	*	*	(4)
IF-3 (condition)	< 65	*	*	(4)
IF-3 (condition)	>= 65	*	*	(3)

Note: The above chart is simply all of the decisions (from the decision-coverage chart) merged with all of the conditions (from the condition-coverage chart) and then minimizing the number of test cases.

Multiple condition coverage	Age	Sex	Married	Test case
IF-1	< 25	Male	True	(1) 23 M T
IF-1	< 25	Male	False	(2) 23 M F
IF-1	< 25	Female	True	(3) 23 F T
IF-1	< 25	Female	False	(4) 23 F F
IF-1	>= 25	Male	True	(5) 30 M T
IF-1	>= 25	Male	False	(6) 70 M F
IF-1	>= 25	Female	True	(7) 50 F T
IF-1	>= 25	Female	False	(8) 30 F F
IF-2	*	Male	True	(5)
IF-2	*	Male	False	(6)
IF-2	*	Female	True	(7)
IF-2	*	Female	False	(8)
IF-3	<= 45, >= 65	*	*	impossible
IF-3	<= 45, < 65	*	*	(8)
IF-3	> 45, >= 65	*	*	(6)
IF-3	> 45, < 65	*	*	(7)

Validation activities

Validation activities can be divided into the following:

(1) Low-level testing
    (i) unit (module) testing
    (ii) integration testing.
(2) High-level testing
    (i) usability testing
    (ii) function testing
    (iii) system testing
    (vi) acceptance testing.

Low-level testing

Low-level testing involves testing individual program components, one at a time or in combination. It requires intimate knowledge of the program's internal structure and is therefore most appropriately performed by development.

Forms of low-level testing are:

- unit (module) testing
- integration testing.

Unit (module) testing

Unit or module testing is the process of testing the individual components (subprograms or procedures) of a program. The purpose is to discover discrepancies between the module's interface specification and its actual behavior.

Unit testing manages the combinations of testing. It facilitates error diagnosis and correction by development and it allows parallelism, in other words, testing multiple components simultaneously.

Testing a given module (X) in isolation may require:

(1) a driver module which transmits test cases in the form of input arguments to X and either prints or interprets the results produced by X;

(2) zero or more "stub" modules each of which simulates the function of a module called by X. It is required for each module that is directly subordinate to X in the execution hierarchy. If X is a terminal module (i.e., it calls no other modules), then no stubs are required.

Integration testing

Integration testing is the process of combining and testing multiple components together. The primary objective of integration testing is to discover errors in the interfaces between the components.

Integration testing can be performed on several levels. We can integrate and test the various modules of a program, the programs of a subsystem, the subsystems of a system, the systems of a network, and so on. There are a number of alternatives in integration testing.

In non-incremental "big bang" integration, all components are combined at once to form the program. The integrated result is then tested. While often used in practice, it is one of the least effective approaches. Debugging is difficult since an error can be associated with any component.

Incremental integration is where we unit test the next program component after combining it with the set of previously tested components. There are two approaches to incremental integration: bottom-up and top-down. Incremental integration has a number of advantages. It requires less work in the sense of fewer driver or stub modules. Errors involving mismatched component interfaces will be detected earlier. Debugging is easier because errors found are usually associated with the most recently added component. More thorough testing may result, because the testing of each new component can provide further function and logic coverage of previously integrated components.

The steps in bottom-up integration are:

- Begin with the terminal modules (those that do not call other modules) of the hierarchy.
- A driver module is produced for every module.
- The next module to be tested is any module whose subordinate modules (the modules it calls) have all been tested.
- After a module has been tested, its driver is replaced by an actual module (the next one to be tested) and its driver.

The steps in top-down integration are:

- Begin with the top module in the execution hierarchy.
- Stub modules are produced, and some may require multiple versions.
- Stubs are often more complicated than they first appear.
- The next module to be tested is any module with at least one previously tested superordinate (calling) module.
- After a module has been tested, one of its stubs is replaced by an actual module (the next one to be tested) and its required stubs.

Bottom-up integration has the disadvantage that the program as a whole does not exist until the last module is added. Top-down integration has the advantage that a skeletal version of the program can exist early and allows demonstrations. However, for top-down integration, the required stubs could be expensive. There is no clear winner here; the advantages of one are the disadvantages of the other, and the choice for testing is often based on the choice made for development.

Here again is an opportunity to take risk management into consideration. An effective alternative is to use a hybrid of bottom-up and top-down, prioritizing the integration of modules based on risk; e.g., the modules associated with the highest risk functions are integration tested earlier in the process than modules associated with low risk functions. Although there is a human tendency to want to do the easy things first, this hybrid approach advises just the opposite.

There are still other incremental integration strategies, which are usually variants of top-down and bottom-up (see References section at the end of the chapter for more details).

High-level testing

High-level testing involves testing whole, complete products. For purposes of objectivity, it is most appropriately performed outside the development organization, usually by an independent test group. Forms of high-level testing are:

- usability testing
- function testing
- system testing
- acceptance testing.

Usability testing

As computers become more affordable, software products are targeted at a larger user base. User expectations are steadily increasing and product purchases are increasingly based on usability. The goal is to adapt software to users' actual work styles, rather than forcing users to adapt their work styles to the software. Testing software for usability is an old idea whose time has come.

Usability testing involves having the users work with the product and observing their responses to it. Unlike Beta testing, which also involves the user, it should be done as early as possible in the development cycle. The real customer is involved as early as possible, even at the stage when only screens drawn on paper are available. The existence of the functional design specification is the prerequisite for starting.

Like all testing, it's important that our objectives are defined. How easy is it for users to bring up what they want? How easily can they navigate through the menus? We should try to do usability testing two or three times during the life cycle (see Figure 8.4).

Usability testing is the process of attempting to identify discrepancies between the user interfaces of a product and the human engineering requirements of its potential users. Testing of the user documentation is an essential component. Usability testing collects information on specific issues from the intended users. It often involves evaluation of a product's presentation rather than its functionality.

Historically, usability testing has been one of many components of system testing because it is requirements-based. Today, its importance and its pervasiveness throughout the development cycle have elevated it to a more prominent role.

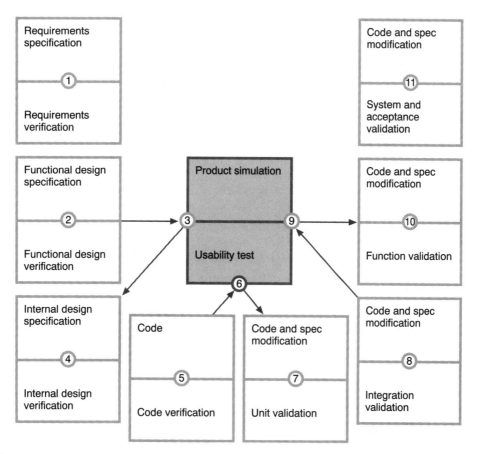

Figure 8.4 The SDT Dotted-U Model, usability test. (© 1993, 1994 Software Development Technologies)

Usability testing is considered a validation activity rather than a verification activity, because it requires a real user to interact with the end product by executing it in either a simulated or a real form. Usability characteristics which can be tested include the following:

- *Accessibility*: Can users enter, navigate, and exit with relative ease?
- *Responsiveness*: Can users do what they want, when they want, in a way that's clear?
- *Efficiency*: Can users do what they want in a minimum amount of steps and time?
- *Comprehensibility*: Do users understand the product structure, its help system, and the documentation?

The usability test process is as follows:

- Define the objectives of the test.
- Define the subjects precisely and recruit them.
- Plan the tests and develop all necessary materials.
- Put subjects in a workroom or lab with their workstations, possibly using video cameras, and a one-way window to an observation room.
- Conduct the test.
- Using video cameras and/or human observers, record the subject's every word and gesture.
- Experts and developers analyze results and recommend changes.

Types of usability tests include the following:

- *Freeform tasks*: Any unplanned task by a user.
- *Structured procedure scripts*: Pre-defined, written scripts containing step-by-step instructions for the user to follow.
- *Paper screens*: The researcher plays the role of computer for the user before any prototype or mock-up is available.
- *Prototype mock-ups*: Using a preliminary prototype rather than the final product.
- *Field trials in the user's office*: Using a prototype or the final product in the user's office.

Usability test methods can be obtrusive when a researcher, or an automated module in the product itself, guides the subject through a script and asks questions. They are unobtrusive when the user works alone or the usability professionals remain silent behind the one-way window.

Function testing

Function testing is the process of attempting to detect discrepancies between a program's functional specification and its actual behavior. When a discrepancy is detected, either the program or the specification could be incorrect. All black-box methods for function-based testing are applicable (see Figure 8.5).

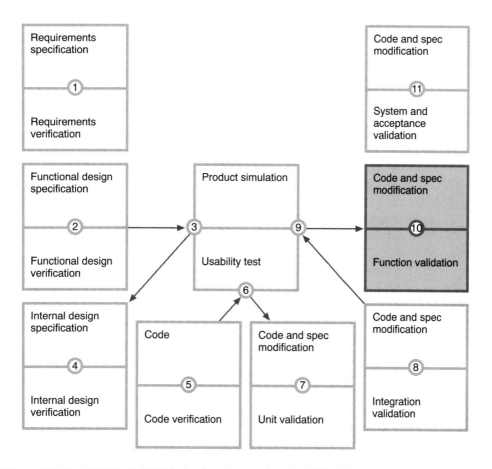

Figure 8.5 The SDT Dotted-U Model, function testing. (© 1993, 1994 Software Development Technologies)

Function testing is performed by a testing group before the product is made available to customers. It can begin whenever the product has sufficient functionality to execute some of the tests, or after unit and integration testing have been completed.

Function coverage is measured as follows:

The execution of a given test case against program P will exercise (cover) certain parts of P's external functionality. A measure of testedness for P is the degree of function coverage produced by the collective set of test cases for P. Function coverage can be measured with a function coverage matrix. Black-box testing methods are used to increase function coverage.

The steps of function testing are:

- Decompose and analyze the functional design specification.
- Partition the functionality into logical components and for each component, make a list of the detailed functions.
- For each function, use the analytical black-box methods to determine inputs and outputs.
- Develop the functional test cases.
- Develop a function coverage matrix.
- Execute the test cases and measure logic coverage.
- Develop additional functional tests, as indicated by the combined logic coverage of function and system testing.

A function coverage matrix (Figure 8.6) is simply a matrix or table listing specific functions to be tested, the priority for testing each function, and the test cases that contain tests for each function.

System testing

System testing is the most misunderstood and the most difficult testing activity. Despite its name, system testing is not the process of function testing the completely integrated system or program. Given function testing, this would be redundant. System testing is the process of attempting to demonstrate that a program or system does not meet its original requirements and objectives, as stated in the requirements specification.

System testing is difficult. There can be no design methodologies for test cases because requirements and objectives do not, and should not, describe the program's functions in precise terms. Requirements must be specific enough to be testable but general enough to allow freedom in the functional design. The specificity necessary for rigorous, universally applicable, technical methods is absent in a requirements specification (see Figure 8.7).

Because there is no methodology, system testing requires a great deal of creativity. We have to keep thinking from the perspective of the user, and the problem the user is trying to solve. System tests are designed by analyzing the requirements specification and then formulated by analyzing the functional design specification or user documentation. This is an ideal way to test user documentation, but it is often impractical because the manuals are usually not available when system test cases must be formulated.

Instead of using a special methodology, we can use various categories of system test cases. Requirements coverage can be stated as follows:

The execution of a given test case against program P will address (cover) certain requirements of P. A measure of testedness for P is the degree of requirements coverage produced by the collective set of test cases for P.

Functions/inputs	Priority	Test cases

Figure 8.6 Function coverage matrix form. (© 1993, 1994 Software Development Technologies)

Black-box testing methods are used to increase requirements coverage. Requirements coverage can be measured with a requirements coverage matrix or a requirements tracing matrix.

Types/goals of system testing are as follows:

- *Volume testing*: to determine whether the program can handle the required volumes of data, requests, etc.
- *Load/stress testing*: to identify peak load conditions at which the program will fail to handle required processing loads within required time spans.
- *Security testing*: to show that the program's security requirements can be subverted.
- *Usability (human factors) testing*: to identify those operations that will be difficult or inconvenient for users. Publications, facilities, and manual procedures are tested.
- *Performance testing*: to determine whether the program meets its performance requirements.
- *Resource usage testing*: to determine whether the program uses resources (memory, disk space, etc.) at levels which exceed requirements.
- *Configuration testing*: to determine whether the program operates properly when the software or hardware is configured in a required manner.

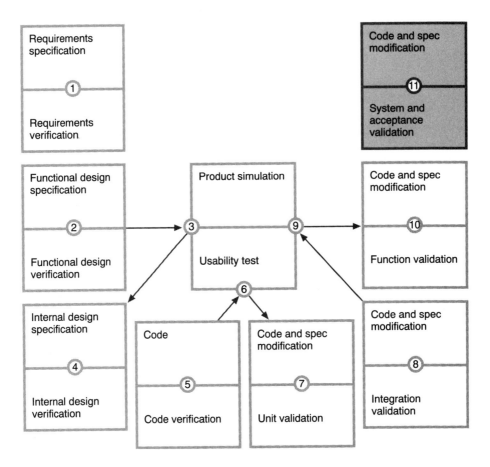

Figure 8.7 The SDT Dotted-U Model, system testing. (© 1993, 1994 Software Development Technologies)

- *Compatibility/conversion testing*: to determine whether the compatibility objectives of the program have been met and whether the conversion procedures work.
- *Installability testing*: to identify the ways in which the installation procedures lead to incorrect results.
- *Recovery testing*: to determine whether the system or program meets its requirements for recovery after a failure.
- *Serviceability testing*: to identify conditions whose serviceability needs will not meet requirements.
- *Reliability/availability testing*: to determine whether the system meets its reliability and availability requirements.

System testing is performed by a testing group before the product is made available to customers. It can begin whenever the product has sufficient functionality to execute some of the tests or after unit and integration testing are completed. It can be conducted in parallel with function testing. Because the tests usually depend on functional interfaces, it may be wise to delay system testing until function testing has demonstrated some pre-defined level of reliability, e.g., 40% of the function testing is complete.

The steps of system testing are:

- Decompose and analyze the requirements specification.
- Partition the requirements into logical categories and, for each component, make a list of the detailed requirements.
- For each type of system testing:
  - For each relevant requirement, determine inputs and outputs.
  - Develop the requirements test cases.
- Develop a requirements coverage matrix which is simply a table in which an entry describes a specific subtest that adds value to the requirements coverage, the priority of that subtest, the specific test cases in which that subtest appears.
- Execute the test cases and measure logic coverage.
- Develop additional tests, as indicated by the combined coverage information.

Acceptance testing
Acceptance testing is the process of comparing the end product to the current needs of its end users. It is usually performed by the customer or end user after the testing group has satisfactorily completed usability, function, and system testing. It usually involves running and operating the software in production mode for a pre-specified period (see Figure 8.8).

If the software is developed under contract, acceptance testing is performed by the contracting customer. Acceptance criteria are defined in the contract. If the product is not developed under contract, the developing organization can arrange for alternative forms of acceptance testing – ALPHA and BETA.

ALPHA and BETA testing are each employed as a form of acceptance testing. Often both are used, in which case BETA follows ALPHA. Both involve running and operating the software in production mode for a pre-specified period. The ALPHA test is usually performed by end users inside the developing company but outside the development organization. The BETA test is usually performed by a selected subset of actual customers outside the company, before the software is made available to all customers.

The first step in implementing ALPHA and BETA is to define the primary objective of the test: *progressive testing*, and/or *regressive testing*. Progressive testing is the process of testing new code to determine whether it contains errors. Regressive testing is the process of testing a program to determine whether a change has introduced errors (regressions) in the unchanged code.

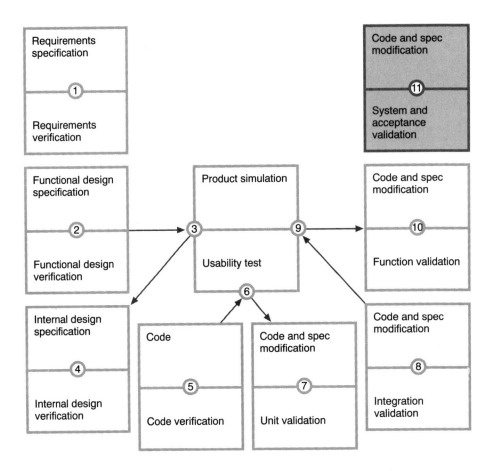

Figure 8.8 The SDT Dotted-U Model, acceptance testing. (© 1993, 1994 Software Development Technologies)

Both ALPHA and BETA are often more effective as regressive, rather than progressive, tests. Both ALPHA and BETA require careful selection of users. Users should be motivated to use the product. Users provide good coverage of hardware and software configurations. Site location is important for support purposes.

You should give careful consideration to the duration of the test. It must be long enough to get the desired feedback. The duration depends on whether or not the new software has an associated learning curve or requires new development by users.

Bilateral plans and agreements are recommended. The user agrees to the duration of the test period and to specified amounts and types of usage during the period and agrees to report problems, progress, and status in a timely fashion. The provider agrees to special support arrangements. Some organizations offer a financial bonus on finding defects of high severity.

Retesting

Why retest? Because any software product that is actively used and supported must be changed from time to time, and every new version of a product should be retested.

Progressive testing and regressive testing

Most test cases, unless they are truly throw-away, begin as progressive test cases and eventually become regression test cases for the life of the product. Regression testing is not another testing activity. It is a re-execution of some or all of the tests developed for a specific testing activity. It may be performed for each activity (e.g., unit test, usability test, function test, system test, etc.).

New versions of a product submitted for testing will be one of the following:

(1) The initial input to a new round of testing, ultimately resulting in a major new version of the product.

(2) A subsequent update to the initial input, regardless of whether it has been made available to customers (i.e., has satisfied its release criteria), or not.

In theory, a subsequent update requires just as much retesting as the initial input, although both of these can introduce serious regressions. Treating them differently involves risk. This risk can be reduced by managing change carefully with configuration management, and understanding the effects of a given change on the product.

Two testing policies at opposite extremes are:

(1) The testing organization, in the spirit of teamwork, agrees to test preliminary and perhaps incomplete versions of a product that are not candidates for general release. Here testing procedures are typically informal. Formal retesting will usually be required when the product is declared a candidate for release. Such a policy could be the target of much abuse of the test organization, which spends all of its time in this mode instead of building an automated regression test library.

(2) The testing organization will accept for testing only those versions of a product that are identified as candidates for release to customers. This is a bit heavy-handed, but sometimes necessary.

In some organizations, the testing function will not accept a product for testing until that product has successfully passed a pre-defined set of acceptance tests. Such acceptance tests are carefully selected to ensure that subsequent testing activities will be productive. This means that the product's basic functions are sufficiently sound so that there is a good probability that all other tests can be executed without major obstructions.

While it may be very helpful to the product development team, executing tests against an incomplete product will usually require the skills and expertise of the test developers. If test developers spend all of their time executing tests, there is no time left for developing more tests. It is important to consider all aspects, including the schedules and economics of the situation, before committing to test products that are not candidates for release. Many testing organizations have rigid criteria for entry of a product into testing (i.e., criteria for acceptance by the testing organization).

Designing for test execution

When designing test cases intended to detect errors, there are test-execution considerations to keep in mind:

- many small test cases vs. a few large ones
- dependencies among test cases
- host environment for test execution
- testpoints.

A test case contains one or more subtests and the objective of every subtest is to detect errors. A subtest might be passing to the product under test:

- valid inputs exclusively
- invalid inputs exclusively
- a combination of valid and invalid inputs.

When a test case causes a failure, a number of things could occur, depending on the test case itself, the test environment, and the product under test. The execution of the test case can be prematurely terminated, in which case the subsequent subtests are not executed. This means that the subsequent subtests can't be executed until the error is corrected or the test case is modified. Alternatively, the execution of the test case can continue as though no failure had occurred.

Test conditions can be masked on several levels:

(1) *Inter-test case*: When one test case (X) depends on another (Y), then when Y cannot satisfy X's dependency because Y caused a failure, the remainder of X may not be executed.

(2) *Intra-test case, inter-subtest*: Within a single test case, when one subtest causes a failure, the remaining subtests may not be executed.

(3) *Intra-subtest, inter-input*: Within a single subtest, when one input causes a failure, the remaining inputs may not be tested.

Example of masking test conditions

- In testing a programmatic interface, a subtest invokes one of the product's procedures (XYZ):

    CALL XYZ (invalid, valid, invalid, valid, invalid);

- XYZ will check the validity of its input parameters in some order that is usually unknown to the tester.
- When the first invalid parameter is detected, XYZ will terminate execution prematurely by either aborting or returning an error code to the caller, leaving all other invalid parameters unchecked.

Note that the above example permanently masks input conditions. Even a valid input, when it creates a failure in the product being tested, can temporarily mask other input conditions until the error is corrected.

Guidelines for test execution

- Use large test cases for subtests using valid inputs.
- Use one test case per subtest using one invalid input.
- A test case can depend on another program but should not depend on another test case.
- The state of the host system should be identical when the execution of each test case is initiated.
- New files should not accumulate.
- Operating modes should not change. This guideline is related to the repeatability of each test case. When a test case causes a failure, it is often difficult to diagnose the cause. The cause can be even further obscured by allowing the underlying environment to get out of control. This guideline is also applicable at the subtest level within a test case.

Testpoints

It is sometimes difficult for test cases to create the conditions necessary for comprehensively testing a product. To overcome these obstacles, testing may ask development to add testpoints to the product. A testpoint is a permanent point in the product which:

- interrogates the value of a variable which can be set via external means by the tester, either manually or programmatically;
- performs one or more specific actions, as indicated by the value of the variable;
- does nothing if the variable is set to its default value.

Testpoints are used to halt the system to test recovery procedures, to introduce timing delays, to invoke a procedure supplied by the tester, and to generate an input/output error condition in a channel, controller, or device to test recovery procedures.

Recommended strategy for validation testing

- Methodically identify, design, and develop function-based tests for function testing, and using black-box methods and requirements-based tests for usability and system testing.
- Run the tests and, using an automated tool, measure their collective internal logic coverage.
- Using white-box methods, methodically identify and develop supplementary internals-based tests as necessary to improve internal logic coverage.
- Review and analyze test results.
- Intensify the testing of any area that exhibits a disproportionately high number of errors.

Externals-based testing should be undertaken by people who have no knowledge of the internal structure of the program to be tested. Such knowledge would bias the tests and can be avoided either by using different people to design the different types of tests, or by using the same people but designing the internals-based tests after the externals-based tests.

- Key black-box methods for function-based testing
    - Equivalence partitioning
    - Boundary-value analysis
    - Error guessing

- White-box methods for internals-based testing
    - Statement coverage
    - Decision coverage
    - Decision/condition coverage
    - Multiple condition coverage

Figure 8.9   Methodology summary. (© 1993, 1994 Software Development Technologies)

Type of testing	Performed by
• Low-level testing	
– Unit (module) testing	Development
– Integration testing	Development
• High-level testing	
– Usability testing	Independent test organization
– Function testing	Independent test organization
– System testing	Independent test organization
– Acceptance testing	Customers

Figure 8.10   Activity summary. (© 1993, 1994 Software Development Technologies)

References

Sources of more detailed information on the analytical methods of black-box and white-box testing and for more detailed information on unit testing, integration testing, and system testing:

Beizer, B. (1984). *Software System Testing and Quality Assurance.* Van Nostrand Rheinhold.

Beizer, B. (1990). *Software Testing Techniques.* Van Nostrand Rheinhold.

Myers, G.J. (1976). *Software Reliability: Principles and Practices.* John Wiley.

Myers, G.J. (1979). *The Art of Software Testing.* John Wiley.

For additional information on usability testing, see:

Myers, G.J., Brad, A. and Rosson, Mary Beth (1993). "Survey on User Interface Programming," *CHI '92 Conference Proceedings.* ACM Conference on Human Factors in Computing Systems.

Rosenbaum, Stephanie (1993). "Alternative Methods for Usability Testing," *Software Testing, Analysis, & Review (STAR) Conference Proceedings.*

Refer also to:
- SIGCHI (ACM Special Interest Group on Human Factors in Computing Systems)
- Usability Professionals Association

Organizations specializing in usability testing:
- American Insitutes for Research, Palo Alto, CA
- IBM User Interface Institute
- Mead Data Central, Inc, Miamisburg, OH
- Multimedia Research, Bellport, NY
- Usability Sciences Corp., Dallas, TX

Chapter 9
Controlling validation costs

If we had unlimited resources we could do all the testing we wanted. In the real world of software projects, we are almost always short of time or money – or both. The discomforting side of it is that not only do we not know how to reduce the costs on a systematic basis, but also we often don't know what the real cost of our testing is in the first place.

Discovering what the real costs are is only possible through measurement (see Chapter 12). But how do we get the costs we have – particularly the validation costs – under the kind of control we are aiming to establish for our testing practices in general? This chapter addresses the main considerations for building cost control into the overall testing strategy.

An important element is testware. Testware is the collection of major work products (deliverables) of testing. The primary objective of testware is to maximize the testing yield, by maximizing the potential for detecting errors and minimizing the number of tests required.

There are additional objectives of testware unrelated to error detection as such, that are extremely important to cost control. These objectives are to minimize the cost of performing tests, the cost of test maintenance, and the cost of test development.

Minimizing the cost of performing tests

The one-time costs of performing tests as progressive tests are usually not very important. The recurring cost of performing these same tests as regression tests for each new version of the product throughout its lifetime is important in proportion to expected need – and that's usually very important.

Cost components in performing tests include:

- pre-run setup cost
- execution cost
- post-run cost.

Pre-run setup costs

Here we are concerned about minimizing the amount of time, the amount of labor, and in particular the amount of skilled labor required to do various essential tasks. These include configuring the hardware, configuring the software, establishing the test environment (restoring files and initialization), and identifying the tests to be run.

Execution costs

Here we aim to minimize the total execution time and dedicated equipment required. Execution time includes attended time (any part of the test execution that requires a manual action by the user or operator where we need to minimize time, labor and skills) plus unattended time.

What are we going to do when we have to re-run our tests? Are we going to run them all each time? These choices are the main engine for cost control in this area, and the decision is based on risk versus cost considerations.

Full regression testing (running all tests) minimizes the risk but increases the cost of test execution. Partial regression testing (running a selected subset of tests) reduces the cost of test execution but increases the risk.

The cost of selecting the right tests for partial regression testing could be high and should be weighed against the reduced cost of test execution. This is dependent on the particular environment. If it is highly automated, sometimes it is cost effective to run all the tests again.

There are two ways to select tests for partial regression testing:

(1) identify and select all tests that would retest everything affected by the change, or
(2) identify and select tests that would retest only those things closely and directly related to the change, knowing that the selection process is less than perfect.

Note that there is less risk associated with (1). Also note that (2) is very subjective, and may still require a significant amount of product knowledge. The general recommendation is to use partial regression testing only if full regression testing is prohibitive.

Post-run costs

Here we aim to minimize the amount of time and the amount of skilled labor required for the analysis and documentation of test results, and for tear-down of the test environment and the restoration of the previous environment.

Recommendations for minimizing the cost of performing tests

Reconfiguring hardware can be time consuming and expensive. When it comes to pre-run, consider the use of dedicated hardware that is permanently configured for the test environment. Automate the configuration of the software and the test environment as much as possible, and, to the extent possible, automate the process of identifying and selecting the tests to be run.

Test execution should be automated as far as possible so as to require no manual assistance. If some portion of the test execution must be attended, it's better to use a junior technician than the test developer. On the other hand, a test developer, repeatedly faced with the task of attending test execution, will usually discover a way to automate it!

When it comes to post-run, to the extent possible, the comparison of test results with expected results should be automated to minimize analysis cost. There are two basic methods for automating tests:

(1) use a testing tool (using an existing tool is almost always more cost effective than building one);

(2) build the automation into the test case itself.

The two recommended candidates for automation are:

(1) manual interactions (by a user or by the system operator) required during execution;

(2) checking of test results.

Both methods apply to both candidates.

Using tools to automate tests

We can use capture/replay tools to automate the execution of tests. In post-run we should automate as much as possible. Taking three days, after the tests have all been run, to manually go through test results before we know whether the software has passed or failed the tests makes little sense given the time pressure that usually prevails at this point. Automation at this stage also eliminates human error.

To automate the checking of test results, use capture/replay or a script-driven simulator during execution and a comparator after execution. There is further and more general material on testing tools and specific information on capture/playback tools in Chapter 11.

Automating manual interactions

Automating manual interaction is desirable for the testing of any software. It is imperative for testing products with highly interactive user interfaces, for simultaneous usage of multi-user software, and for software with graphic user interfaces (GUIs).

The basic categories of manual actions are operator actions, which advance the execution of the tests, such as mounting a tape, initiating or resuming execution, and user actions required by interactive, script-driven testing.

Automating checking of test results is desirable for all tests because, in addition to eliminating manual work, it reinforces the need to pre-define the expected results. Depending on test case design, test results can be checked in two ways:

(1) During execution (on the fly) – an exception message is printed when actual and expected results disagree.

(2) After execution – actual test results are written to a file during execution and compared with expected results after execution.

Minimizing the cost of maintaining the tests

Regression tests should be faithfully maintained for the life of the software product. Like the software components for the product itself, all testware components should be placed under the control of a configuration management system.

The key maintenance tasks are:

- add a test for each confirmed problem reported;
- add progressive tests to test new changes;
- periodically review all test cases for continued effectiveness.

How do we determine the continued effectiveness of tests?

(1) *Each test case should be executable*; that is, the product being tested should not have introduced functional changes which prevent the intended execution of the test case.

(2) *Requirements-based and function-based tests should be valid*; that is, a change in product requirements or functionality should not have rendered the test case misleading (detecting errors that don't exist) or useless (failing to detect errors that it used to detect).

(3) *Each test case should continue to add value*; that is, it should not be completely redundant with another test case, but it may often be more cost effective to continue using it than to determine its added value.

To preserve their customers' investment in their products, many software producers commit to providing upward compatible functionality in each new release. This commitment can be exploited by the tester by maximizing the number of tests that use only those interfaces described in the functional specification. This applies to all tests, even requirements-based and internals-based tests. Such tests should serve as useful, maintenance-free regression tests for all releases of the product.

For usability reasons, software producers often make significant, incompatible changes in user interfaces of products from one release to the next. Such changes are usually in the interactive, as opposed to programmatic, interfaces of products. Such changes may be good for users, even considering the (usually small) cost of retraining.

However, these changes create more work (but provide job security) for testers. New tests must be developed. Old tests must be examined and affected tests must be changed or declared obsolete. Where there is a clear one-for-one change in a product interface, a good tool or a one-off conversion program might be able to modify the corresponding tests automatically.

There is a dark side to white-box testing. A test case that references a product interface for which there is no (expressed or implied) commitment to future compatibility is a high maintenance test case – invoking internal procedures directly, and/or examining or setting an internal data item. The number of such test cases should be minimized because they must be re-examined for continued validity prior to each use. Use this kind of testing carefully, but use it when it is needed. At the same time, try to get commitments to maintain compatibility for the future.

Axioms for test maintenance

The axioms for test maintenance are:

- Never alter a program to make the testing of that program easier (e.g., testing hooks), unless it is a permanent change.
- If a test case must reference an internal item in a product, always try to extract a commitment from development to make that item permanent.

Minimizing validation testware development costs

For validation testing, testware includes test cases and test data as well as supporting documentation such as test plans, test specifications, test procedures, and test reports.

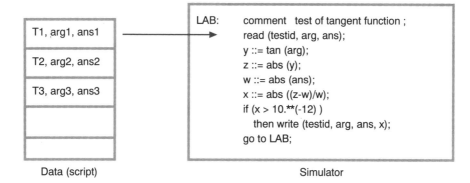

Figure 9.1   Example of a script-driven simulation test. Real (floating point) numbers will seldom be exactly equal. So the test for equality is described in the algorithm (asking whether their first 12 decimal digits are equal). (© 1993, 1994 Software Development Technologies)

The development of quality testware requires the same disciplines as are applied to good software engineering in general. We have to plan each stage, and understand what is required before the design begins. We need a detailed design before coding begins and we must comply with established coding standards. We should use inspections and walkthroughs on testware, as we would on any other important software product. Test users will need user documentation. Overall, testware should be treated as the important business asset that it is by placing it under control of a configuration management system.

The basic testware acquisition strategies are, quite simply, build, buy or reuse. Testware should always be reused if possible, which is why the maintenance of testware is so important.

Buy testware if it is available. For some standards-based software, appropriate testware can be purchased fairly easily (e.g., validation tests for C, UNIX, COBOL, Pascal). Sometimes useful test libraries can be bought from companies doing the same kind of work. Build testware only if absolutely necessary, because it is usually the least cost-effective solution. It can be built in-house, or by an outside contractor. Another important consideration in developing testware is the cost of automating execution versus the cost of executing non-automated tests, and the use of existing test tools.

Some types of software products or product-components lend themselves to testing via a script-driven simulator. Actual tests and their expected results are written and stored as data records (scripts) in a text file. One program (a simulator) is written, and it reads the data for each test, interprets and executes it, and compares the actual to the expected results.

Writing tests as data rather than as code can reduce development (and maintenance) costs. The larger the number of tests, the greater the savings. This is most useful when testing programmatic interfaces (see Figure 9.1).

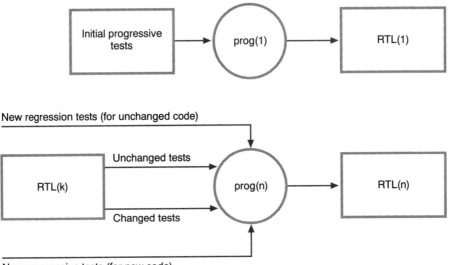

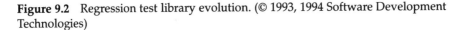

Figure 9.2   Regression test library evolution. (© 1993, 1994 Software Development Technologies)

The testware library

Because testware must be accessed frequently, test cases should be organized and cataloged in the form of a library for convenient access. Over the life of the testware, such a library affords significant cost savings in performing tests and maintaining them. An easy-to-use testware library will be used to advantage by others, not just its creators. A library should be organized in such a way that all test cases or any subset can be selected and executed with minimal effort (see Figure 9.2).

Define a structure and naming conventions that are most appropriate for the organization's particular testing needs. To make the library useful to others, collect related test cases that are normally run as a unit into (named) groups. A test library may contain many groups, and any given test case belongs to one or more groups.

The library structure and/or grouping and naming conventions should explicitly identify and differentiate:

- test cases and groups that require the same execution environment;
- high-maintenance tests that must be examined prior to each use;
- the nature (category, purpose, test-basis) of the test case or group.

The test library should contain:

- an index or roadmap;
- a description of the library structure and grouping and naming conventions;
- for each test group:
  - a description of the group and grouping criteria
  - the names of the test cases in the group
  - test procedure documentation (for the group)
  - a command file to execute all test cases in the group;
- for each test case:
  - test case and test procedure documentation
  - all associated files (source, object, data, etc), including a command file to execute the test case and command files to create all derived files.

Recommendations

- Review how accurate your information is on your present test spending.
- Evaluate the use of dedicated hardware that is permanently configured for the test environment.
- Automate the comparison of test results with expected results to minimize analysis cost.
- Investigate using capture/replay tools to automate test execution.
- Place all testware components under the control of a configuration management system.
- Plan a periodical review of all test cases for continued effectiveness.

Chapter 10

Testing tasks, deliverables, and chronology

Effective testing is planned. Successful testing requires a methodical approach involving discipline, structure, analysis, and measurement. Unorganized, shotgun, random approaches will almost always fail.

Each testing activity has one or more inputs (development or documentation deliverables) and consists of one or more tasks. Each task produces one or more outputs (testing deliverables).

This chapter describes the specific tasks and the deliverables associated with each testing activity, and the standards which provide help with these tasks and deliverables. It includes an outline for the content of each deliverable document, and where applicable, a reference to the IEEE/ANSI standard for the document. These tasks and deliverables are mapped into specific phases of the software life cycle, showing their relative timing and overlap.

Time and resources almost always limit the testing we can do in practice. At every level of testing (activity, task, subtask, etc.) it is important to set priorities on every aspect of the work being considered. The main basis for setting these priorities is risk.

Master test planning

An overview of testing tasks is as follows:

(1) Master test planning task
(2) Verification testing tasks (per activity)
    (i)   planning
    (ii) execution
(3) Validation testing tasks (per activity)
    (i)   planning
    (ii) testware development
    (iii) test execution
    (iv) testware maintenance.

The master test planning risk management considerations include:

- size and complexity of the product to be tested;
- criticality of the product. Critical software is software in which a failure could have an impact on safety or could cause large financial or social losses (IEEE/ANSI, 1986 [Std 1012-1986]);
- (SEI) development process maturity level;
- form of testing (full, partial, endgame, audit);
- staffing, experience, and organization.

(See Chapter 5 for more detail on the background to these considerations.)

A three-level priority scheme (LO, MED, HI) is usually sufficient. When the work is being performed the HI priority items are done first, then MED, and then, if time permits, LO.

In master test planning the aim is to get the big picture clear in a high-level document – a master schedule, master resource usage, a master life cycle, and quality assurance issues to be addressed. What kind of testing will we be doing? How much verification? What kind of validation? Do we do accept-ance testing? What overall strategy will we need?

One such "big picture" deliverable is the software verification and validation plan. Performing software verification and validation, as defined in the IEEE/ANSI Standard 1012-1986, provides for a comprehensive evaluation throughout each phase to help ensure that errors are detected and corrected as early as possible in the software life cycle, and project risk, cost, and schedule effects are lessened. Software quality and reliability are enhanced, proposed changes and their consequences can be quickly assessed, and transparency in the software process is improved.

Deliverable: software V&V plan (outline)

(IEEE/ANSI, 1986 [Std 1012-1986])
- Purpose
- Referenced documents
- Definitions
- Verification and validation overview
  - organization, master schedule, resources summary, responsibilities, tools, techniques, and methodologies
- Life-cycle verification and validation
  - tasks, inputs, and outputs per life-cycle phase
- Software verification and validation reporting
  - describes content, format, and timing of all V&V reports
- Verification and validation administrative procedures
  - policies, procedures, standards, practices, conventions

IEEE Standard 1012-1986 contains charts and explanatory information that assist the author in preparing the plan. The overall intent of the plan is to describe the V&V activities that will be applied to the project. The Standard document defines the outline of the plan and basically serves as a checklist for the content of the plan. The software V&V plan is included in the list of minimum documentation requirements for critical software, and it is subordinate to the umbrella software quality assurance plan (SQAP).

The SQAP is the highest level, testing related document. It references the fact that there is a software V&V plan. The software QA plan is directed toward the development and maintenance of critical software; a subset of the standard may be applied to non-critical software. The purpose of the SQAP is to show the user, the developer, and the public the specific measures that are being taken to ensure quality in the software. It includes items such as how configuration management and relationships with suppliers and contractors will be handled. The SQAP is prepared by a SQA group or an appropriate representative body.

Deliverable: software quality assurance plan (outline)

(IEEE/ANSI, 1989 [Std 730-1989])

- Purpose
- Referenced documents
- Management
- Documentation
- Standards, practices, conventions, and metrics
- Life-cycle verification and validation
- Reviews and audits
- Test
- Problem reporting and corrective action
- Tools, techniques, and methodologies
- Code control
- Media control
- Supplier control
- Records collection, maintenance, and retention
- Training
- Risk management

Verification testing tasks and deliverables

An overview of verification activities is as follows:

(1) Activities
    (i)   requirements verification
    (ii) functional design verification
    (iii) internal design verification
    (iv) code verification
(2) Verification tasks (per activity) include:
    (i)   planning
    (ii) execution.

Verification test planning

Are we going to do requirements verification? What methods are we going to use: full-blown formal inspections, or walkthroughs, or desk checks? What areas of the work product will be verified? One hundred per cent of the requirements specified? Fifty per cent of the code? What are the risks involved in not doing it? What is the resource schedule and what are the responsibilities?

Verification test planning considerations include:

- the verification activity to be performed;
- the methods to be used (inspections, walkthroughs, etc.);
- the specific areas of the work product that will and will not be verified;
- the risks associated with any areas of the work product that will not be verified;
- prioritizing the areas of the work product to be verified;
- resources, schedule, facilities, tools, responsibilities.

The deliverables comprise one verification test plan per verification activity. For each verification activity to be performed (i.e., requirements verification, functional design verification, internal design verification, code verification), a verification test plan is produced. Its purpose is to describe in detail how the verification will be performed, the areas of the work product that will and will not be verified, associated risks and priorities, and other standard planning information. There is no IEEE/ANSI standard for this document.

Deliverable: verification test plan (outline)

- Test-plan identifier
- Introduction
- Verification activity (requirements vs. ...)
- Areas to be verified, not verified
- Tasks
- Responsibilities
- Staffing and training needs
- Schedule
- Risks and contingencies
- Approvals

Verification execution

Tasks:
- inspections, walkthroughs, technical reviews

Deliverables:
- inspection report (one per inspection)
- verification test report (one per verification activity)

Each individual inspection delivers a report on its activity. What was inspected? Who was there? How much did people work in advance? What was the error rate? Where were the defects found and in what category of severity? What conclusions did we come to about the product? Do we need to reinspect after the errors have been fixed? Was the whole meeting aborted? Why? How much rework is needed?

Deliverable: inspection report (outline)

- Inspection report identifier
- Test item and version
- Number of participants
- Size of the materials inspected
- Total preparation time of the inspection team
- Disposition of the software element
- Estimate of the rework effort and rework completion date
- Defect list
- Defect summary (number of defects by category)

The inspection report outline was derived from section 6.8 of IEEE/ANSI Standard for Software Reviews and Audits (Std 1028-1988), which sets minimum requirements for report content.

There is one more verification execution-related deliverable, the verification test report. This test report is a summary of verification activities. We aimed to verify 100% of the software related documentation, but how much did we end up actually verifying? What kind of internal issues came up that need resolving? This is what was achieved, this is what was not. It can be seen as an executive summary, which can be used to raise management awareness of the testing process, and draw their attention to issues that need to be addressed.

Deliverable: verification test report (outline)

- Verification report identifier
- Type of verification
- Test item and version
- Summary
- Variances (from requirements at start of phase)
- Internal issues (as a stand-alone entity)
- Log of verification steps (meetings, inspections, special actions, etc.)
- Summary of criticality and risk assessment
- List of open action items

There is one verification test report per work product (not one per inspection meeting). Its purpose is to summarize all the verification steps (tasks) that were performed for this verification activity. There is no IEEE/ANSI standard for this document.

Validation testing tasks and deliverables

A summary of validation activities is as follows:

- Unit testing (by development)
- Usability testing
- Function testing
- System testing
- Acceptance testing

Validation tasks:

- High-level planning for all validation activities as a whole
- Testware architectural design
- Per activity:
  - detailed planning
  - testware development
  - test execution
  - test evaluation
  - testware maintenance

Validation test planning

What kind of test methods are we going to use? What kind of test automation, including tools? What kind of budget do we have? What support software and training do we need? How are we going to do our configuration management?

Validation test planning considerations:

- test methods
- facilities (for testware development vs. test execution)
- test automation
- support software (shared by development and test)
- configuration management
- risks (budget, resources, schedule, training, etc.)

These considerations apply to both the overall testing effort and each individual validation activity (in more detail).

One master validation test plan should be produced for the overall validation testing effort. One or more detailed validation test plans should be produced for each validation activity (unit testing, integration testing, usability testing, function testing, system testing, and acceptance testing).

The purpose of the master validation test plan is to provide an overview of the entire validation testing effort. It should identify the specific validation activities to be performed, the approximate resources required by each, a rough schedule for each, the overall training needs and the risks.

Deliverable: master validation test plan

(IEEE/ANSI, 1983 [Std 829-1983])

Purpose:

- To prescribe the scope, approach, resources, and schedule of the testing activities.

Outline:

- Test-plan identifier
- Introduction
- Test items
- Features to be tested
- Features not to be tested
- Approach
- Item pass/fail criteria
- Suspension criteria and resumption requirements
- Test deliverables
- Testing tasks
- Environmental needs
- Staffing and training needs
- Schedule
- Risks and contingencies
- Approvals

There is at least one detailed (validation test) plan per validation testing activity. The purpose of the detailed plan is to describe in detail how that validation activity will be performed:

- unit testing (by development)
- integration testing (by development)
- usability testing
- function testing
- system testing ·
- acceptance testing.

The test plan outline above may be used for both the master and detailed validation test plans. Every item in the outline is applicable to the detailed test plan where we itemize what we are going to test, the features to be tested, and the features not to be tested. In other words, for the detailed test plan, every item can still apply, but on a lower, more detailed level.

Test architecture design

An important supplement to the master validation test plan is the test architecture design. Architecture design is the process of designing a meaningful and useful structure to the tests as a whole. How do we organize the tests? Are they requirements-based tests, function-based tests, or internals-based tests? How do we categorize them? What is the logical grouping of tests we intend to execute together? How do we structure the test repository?

There is one and only one test architecture specification per major software product. It can be seen as the root document (roadmap) of the entire test repository.

The key architecture design considerations include:

(1) organization of the tests with respect to test basis (requirements- vs. function- vs. internals-based tests);
(2) categorization of the tests and grouping conventions;
(3) structure and naming conventions for the test repository;
(4) grouping of tests for reasonable execution periods.

Deliverable: test-architecture specification

- Test-specification identifier
- Introduction
- Test repository location
- Test repository storage and access conventions
- Test repository structure/organization
- Standards
- Grouping and naming conventions for all files

Testware development – detailed design and implementation

Testware is designed with the following objectives:

- detect as many errors as possible
- minimize test development costs
- minimize test execution costs
- minimize test maintenance cost.

Testware is software, so good software design and software engineering techniques apply to testware development.

The tasks of testware development include:

- detailed design
- implementation.

At this stage we are working towards the test design specification. What are we going to test? What are the priorities assigned to it? How are we going to put together the high-level test designs for groups of related items? How are we going to approach actually doing the tests?

Detailed design is the process of specifying the details of the test approach for a software feature or combination of features and identifying the associated test cases. Detailed design considerations are:

- satisfying test development objectives;
- conforming to the test architecture;
- design of each test case.

The deliverables of detailed design are test design specifications and test case specifications.

The basic steps of detailed test design

- identifying the items that should be tested;
- assigning priorities to these items, based on risk;
- developing high-level test designs for groups of related test items;
- designing individual test cases from the high-level designs.

Test item identification is the process of identifying all target items to be tested. The first step of test item identification is a careful study, decomposition, and analysis of the requirements and functional design specifications. Using black-box methodologies, a list of target test items for function-based tests is developed. A test item is the subject of a subtest. Using experience and ingenuity, we create a separate list of target test items for requirements-based tests for each relevant type of system testing. In some test literature, test items are called test objectives, and the collection of test items is called an inventory.

Anything at our disposal can be used to develop separate lists of test items for requirements-based tests for each type of system test. Any or all of the following types might apply, and may require special approaches to test design, special tools or hardware or environment. For each type of system testing, first consider whether the type is applicable. If it is, develop a list of test items based on the specific requirements for that type of system test.

Types of system tests (for requirements-based tests):

- volume
- usability
- performance
- configuration
- compatibility/conversion
- reliability/availability
- load/stress
- security
- resource usage
- installability
- recovery
- serviceability.

Once again, we can't do everything, but we have to be sure we have done the essentials, and we need to assign priorities (based on risk) to our lists of target test items. Steps for refining the lists of target test items include:

(1) If the lists were developed independently, compare the two lists, and eliminate redundant test items.
(2) Prioritize (LO, MED, HI) the test items on each list, based on schedule, resources, and risk of not testing each item.
(3) For each list, create a coverage matrix which will later (after the actual test cases are identified) show the mapping between test items and test cases (i.e., which test cases cover which test items).
(4) For critical software, create a requirements tracing matrix.

When assessing risk, be aware that an untested condition could prove inconsequential for one customer and disastrous for another because of their different usage patterns.

For critical software, the IEEE/ANSI Standard for Software Verification and Validation Plans (Std 1012-1986) requires:

- requirements traceability analysis
- design traceability analysis
- code traceability analysis.

Requirement	Functional design	Internal design	Code	Tests
Restaurant has two ordering stations	Mgmt screen #2	Page 45	Line 12485	34, 57, 63
A waiter may order from any station	Order screen	Page 19	Line 6215	12, 14, 34, 57, 92
Any customer at a table may request a separate check	Order screen	Page 39	Line 2391	113, 85
A customer may get checks from more than one station	Check printing	Page 138	Lines 49234, 61423	74, 104

Figure 10.1   Example of a requirement tracing matrix. (© 1993, 1994 Software Development Technologies)

These analyses are embodied in the requirements tracing matrix, the purpose of which is to help ensure that for critical software, nothing falls through the cracks (see Figure 10.1). Ultimately there is a way of mapping for each requirement which tests cases exist to cover that requirement and the functional design.

The requirements tracing matrix links each requirement to its destination in the functional design, to its support in the internal design, to its support in the code, and to the set of tests for that requirement. References are re-verified when a change occurs.

For a typical real-world product to be tested, there are usually many test design specifications. The test design specification is a kind of umbrella document that helps identify test cases. The same test case may be identified in more than one test design specification. There are one or more test case specifications per test design specification. In practice, many organizations combine these two documents, eliminating the need for the more detailed test case specifications.

Deliverable: test design specification

(IEEE/ANSI, 1983 [Std 829-1983])

Purpose:

- To specify refinements of the test approach and to identify the features to be covered by the design and its associated tests. It also identifies the test cases and test procedures, if any, required to accomplish the testing and specifies the feature pass/fail criteria.

Outline:

- Test design specification identifier
- Features to be tested
- Approach refinements
- Test case identification
- Feature pass/fail criteria

Deliverable: test case specification

(IEEE/ANSI, 1983 [Std 829-1983])

Purpose:

- To define a test case identified by a test design specification. The test case spec documents the actual values used for input along with the anticipated outputs. It identifies any constraints on the test procedures resulting from use of that specific test case. Test cases are separated from test designs to allow for use in more than one design and to allow for reuse in other situations.

Outline:

- Test case specification identifier
- Test items
- Input specifications
- Output specifications
- Environmental needs
- Special procedural requirements
- Intercase dependencies

Implementation is the process of translating each test case specification into ready-to-execute test cases. The deliverables of implementation are:

- test cases, test data
- test procedure specifications
- completed function-coverage matrix

- completed requirements-coverage matrix
- for critical software, a completed requirements tracing matrix.

The test procedure specification explains step by step how to set up, how to start the tests, how to monitor the test run, and how to restart the tests if they have been suspended. A good written specification is important, so information on running this particular test library isn't just in someone's head.

Deliverable: test procedure specification

(IEEE/ANSI, 1983 [Std 829-1983])

Purpose:

- To identify all steps required to operate the system and exercise the specified test cases in order to implement the associated test design. The procedures are separated from test design specifications as they are intended to be followed step by step and should not have extraneous detail.

Outline:

- Test procedure specification identifier
- Purpose
- Special requirements
- Procedural steps

Test execution

A test execution overview is as follows. Tasks include:

- test case selection
- pre-run setup, execution, post-run analysis
- recording activities, results, and incidents
- determining whether failures are caused by errors in the product or in the tests themselves
- measuring internal logic coverage.

Test execution is the process of executing all or selected test cases and observing the results. Some organizations (those having a more mature test process) require that certain criteria be met before a product is eligible for entry into test (execution). The rationale for such criteria is to prevent the premature testing of a product that isn't ready for testing, and the wasting of time in both development and testing groups.

Example: requirements for entry to test (execution)

- The product is fundamentally complete.
- The product being submitted for test is a candidate for release to customers.
- All appropriate verification activities for this version of the product have been completed.
- All specifications in the derivation chain of the code are approved and frozen with respect to this version of the product.
- A set of "acceptance tests" selected by the test group have been executed without incident. Such acceptance tests are a proper subset of the test repository, and their incident free execution should indicate that the product is sufficiently reliable to make a complete test possible.

The key test execution deliverables are test logs, test incident reports, and the logic coverage report (tool output).

Usability testing may be performed numerous times throughout the development and test cycle. Usability testing is considered a validation activity because it employs real users in a product execution environment (real, simulated or mockup). As such, there may be many usability testing sessions, each of which should produce one test log report and any number of test incident reports.

The test log is the document in which we save the details about the execution of the tests. What do we save? What do we document? How long do we keep it around? It is the kind of information that is useful to refer to if we need to demonstrate whether a problem is a day-one problem or a regression.

Deliverable: test log

(IEEE/ANSI, 1983 [Std 829-1983])

Purpose:

- To provide a chronological record of relevant details about the execution of tests.

Outline:

- Test log identifier
- Description
- Activity and event entries

An incident report is another name for a defect (i.e., problem, bug) report. The most important part of it is the incident description, which should not just describe what happened but should always compare expected results with actual results.

Deliverable: test incident report

(IEEE/ANSI, 1983 [Std 829-1983])

Purpose:

- To document any test execution event which requires further investigation.

Outline:

- Test incident report identifier
- Summary
- Incident description
- Impact

Any incident report, regardless of origin (tester, internal user, customer, etc.) should be assigned a degree of severity by the originator. Severity measures the actual or anticipated impact on the user's operational environment. Standard definitions for severity should be established. No less than three and no more than five levels of severity are recommended.

The notion of severity is valuable in establishing service priorities, in gauging a product's release readiness, and in defining numerous quality metrics. From the point of view of development, the severity of a confirmed problem is a function of two things: the probability that the problem will occur, and the impact of the problem when it does occur. From the point of view of the user who has experienced the problem, usually only the latter is relevant.

Test evaluation

A test evaluation overview is as follows:

- test coverage evaluation
- product error evaluation
- test effectiveness evaluation.

Test coverage evaluation is the process of assessing the thoroughness of the collective set of test cases for the product and deciding whether or not to develop additional tests. The thoroughness assessment is based on current test coverage at various levels; function coverage (use function coverage matrix), requirements coverage (use requirements coverage matrix), logic coverage (using coverage measurement results). The specific deliverables of this effort are additional tests (usually internals-based) as appropriate.

Function coverage and requirements coverage are known prior to test execution. Test coverage analysis cannot be fully completed until test execution provides information on logic coverage. If more tests are required, we loop back into the "detailed design" stage of test development.

Product error evaluation is the process of assessing the quality of the product, with respect to the test execution, and deciding whether or not to develop additional tests. Usually 20% of the code has the lion's share of the errors. The quicker this 20% is located the better, because it is a good indicator of errors remaining. This assessment is based on the number of detected errors, their nature and severity, the areas of the product in which errors were detected and the rate of error detection. The specific deliverables of this effort are additional tests (that may have any test basis), if necessary.

Test effectiveness evaluation is the process of assessing the overall effectiveness of the current testing effort relative to the test completion criteria and deciding whether to stop testing or to add more tests and continue. The effectiveness assessment is based jointly on test coverage evaluation and product error evaluation.

At this point the key issues are:

- Do we decide to stop or continue testing?
- What additional tests are needed, if the decision is to continue?
- How do we create the test summary report, if the decision is to stop?

When do we stop?

The classic test completion criteria are that the clock runs out (i.e., the allocated testing time elapses), or all tests run to completion without detecting any errors.

Fortunately, there are meaningful and useful completion criteria. Ideally they should be based on all of the following components:

(1) The successful use of specific test case design methodologies.
(2) A percentage of coverage for each coverage category.
(3) The rate of error detection (i.e., the number of errors detected per unit of testing time) falls below a specified threshold. A criteria based on the number of detected errors should be qualified by the error severity levels.
(4) The detection of a specific number of errors (a percentage of total errors estimated to exist), or a specific elapsed time.

A model for tracking test execution status

Count the number of test cases in each of the following categories:

- *Planned*: Test cases that planned to be developed.
- *Available*: Planned test cases that are available for execution. (Available is less than or equal to planned.)
- *Executed*: Available test cases that have been executed. (Executed is less than or equal to available.)
- *Passed*: Executed test cases whose most recent executions have detected no errors. (Passed is less than or equal to executed.)

Plot these four numbers periodically (weekly, daily, etc.) against time and analyze the trends.

If test cases are divided into these four categories, a matrix can be set up on a product-by-product basis, and tracked over time, or tracked by ratios like passed/planned ratios. We could, for instance, decide to ship the product only when the passed to plan ratio is over 97%. Graphics on test execution status can provide all sorts of useful curves that can be analyzed to provide good practical test management information (see Figure 10.2).

The final document is the test summary report, in which the results of validation activities are summarized; what was planned, what was achieved in terms of coverage, how many defects were found, and of what severity. It can also be regarded as a report for management on testing activity.

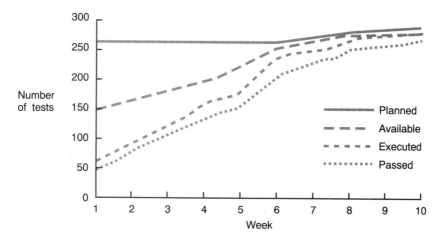

Figure 10.2   Sample test execution graph. (© 1993, 1994 Software Development Technologies)

Deliverable: test summary report

(IEEE/ANSI, 1983 [Std 829-1983])

Purpose:

- To summarize the results of the testing activities associated with one or more test design specifications and to provide evaluations based on these results.

Outline:

- Test summary report identifier
- Summary
- Variances
- Comprehensive assessment
- Summary of results
- Evaluation
- Summary of activities
- Approvals

A testing orphan – user manuals

Every software product that is delivered to a customer consists of both the executable code and the user manuals. A product's documentation is no less important than its code, because its quality is a significant factor in the success or failure of a product. From the point of view of the user, if the manual says do something, and the user follows these instructions and it doesn't work, it doesn't really help that the code is in fact right. Software and testing literature are predominantly silent on the testing of manuals, probably because manuals are usually produced by technical writers (not developers or testers) using life cycles, deliverables, and terminology for which there are no standards.

"User Documentation Evaluation" is defined as an optional task by IEEE/ANSI Standard for Software Verification and Validation Plans (Std 1012-1986). The task can occur in all phases of the development cycle. Documentation may include user manuals or guides, as appropriate to the project.

Examine draft documents during the development process to ensure correctness, understandability, and completeness. Treat manuals as important elements of a product. They should be subjected to a comprehensive testing process, using the concepts and methods of verification, including plans and reports.

Consider employing a critical review process. If the manuals are perceived as equal in importance to the code, then formal inspections are appropriate. Inspect manuals for correctness, understandability, and completeness.

To the degree that the manuals are perceived as less important than the code, then use less formal methods. Use the generic document verification checklist in Appendix B when reviewing manuals.

If the functional design specification is faithfully maintained, then it is the test basis for the manuals because the primary test objective for manuals is to find discrepancies between them. All examples in the manuals should be performed as part of the manuals testing effort to determine if they work as described.

Product release criteria

While most organizations have some kind of release criteria, all too often they are very informal. As companies mature, release criteria become more specific and more measurable. Releasing a new version of a product to customers (any version, not just the first) involves more than satisfactory completion of validation testing. Some typical release criteria are:

- all components of the end product, including user documentation, are complete and tested;
- software release and support policy is defined and understood;
- software manufacturing/distribution is ready;
- software support is ready;
- customers know how to report problems.

Summary of IEEE/ANSI test related documents

The following is a summary of all of the documents used in test planning and specification and how they relate to each other and the various testing activities and the respective standards. See Figures 10.3 and 10.4.

Documentation structure for test planning and specification

SQAP: Software Quality Assurance Plan (IEEE/ANSI, 1989 [Std 730-1989]). One per software product to be tested.

SVVP: Software Verification and Validation Plan (IEEE/ANSI, 1986 [Std 1012-1986]). One per SQAP.

VTP: Verification Test Plan. One per verification activity.

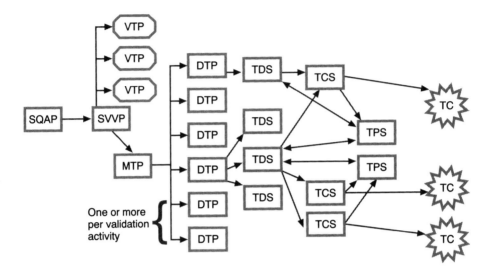

Figure 10.3   Documentation structure for test planning and specification. (© 1993, 1994 Software Development Technologies)

MTP: (Master Validation) Test Plan (IEEE/ANSI, 1983 [Std 829-1983]). One per SVVP.

DTP: (Detailed Validation) Test Plan (IEEE/ANSI, 1983 [Std 829-1983]). One or more per activity.

TDS: Test Design Specification (IEEE/ANSI, 1983 [Std 829-1983]). One or more per DTP.

TCS: Test Case Specification (IEEE/ANSI, 1983 [Std 829-1983]). One or more per TDS/TPS.

TPS: Test Procedure Specification (IEEE/ANSI, 1983 [Std 829-1983]). One or more per TDS.

TC: Test Case. One per TCS.

Documentation structure for test reporting

VTR: Verification Test Report. One per verification activity.

TPS: Test Procedure Specification. (IEEE/ANSI, 1983 [Std 829-1983]).

TL: Test Log (IEEE/ANSI, 1983 [Std 829-1983]). One per testing session.

TIR: Test Incident Report (IEEE/ANSI, 1983 [Std 829-1983]). One per incident.

TSR: Test Summary Report (IEEE/ANSI, 1983 [Std 829-1983]). One.

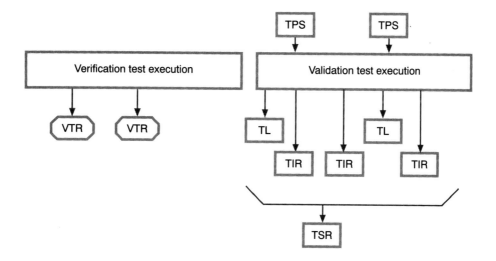

Figure 10.4   Documentation structure for test reporting. (© 1993, 1994 Software Development Technologies)

Life-cycle mapping of tasks and deliverables

This section maps each input, task, and deliverable of testing into its appropriate phase of a software life cycle with the following phases:

- concept
- requirements
- functional design
- internal design
- coding
- integration and test
- operation/maintenance.

The various phases of a life-cycle model may overlap to a considerable extent, but phase completions (approval of deliverables, signoffs, etc.) should occur in a specified sequence. Many of the testing tasks may actually span multiple phases, but they are shown in the earliest possible start phase. Testing deliverables are shown in the latest possible completion (due) phase.

The life-cycle scenario presented here presumes the full form of testing (where testing involvement begins no later than the requirements phase).

Concept phase

(1) *Inputs to testing*
    (i)   Informal project discussions
(2) *Testing tasks*
    (i)   Strategic planning
    (ii) Learn as much as possible about the product and project
(3) *Testware deliverables*
    none

Requirements phase

(1) *Inputs to testing*
    (i)   Software quality assurance plan (optional, from SQA)
    (ii) Requirements (from development)
(2) *Testing tasks*
    (i)   Plan (for verification and validation separately)
    (ii) Analyze the requirements
    (iii) Verify the requirements
    (iv) Begin to identify, itemize, and design requirements-based tests and develop a requirements coverage or tracing matrix
(3) *Testware deliverables*
    (i)   Software V&V plan
    (ii) Verification test plan (for requirements)
    (iii) Verification test report (for requirements)

Functional design phase

(1) *Inputs to testing*
    (i)   Functional design specification (from development)
(2) *Testing tasks*
    (i)   Plan for functional design verification, validation
    (ii) Analyze the functional design specification
    (iii) Verify the functional design specification
    (iv) Begin performing usability tests
    (v) Begin to identify, itemize, and design function-based tests and to develop a function coverage matrix
    (vi) Begin implementation of requirements-based and function-based tests

(3) *Testware deliverables*
- (i)   (Master validation) test plan (IEEE/ANSI, 1983 [Std 829-1983])
- (ii) Verification test plan (for functional design)
- (iii) Verification test report (for functional design)

Internal design phase

(1) *Inputs to testing*
- (i)   Internal design specification (from development)

(2) *Testing tasks*
- (i)   Plan for internal design verification
- (ii) Analyze the internal design specification
- (iii) Verify the internal design specification
- (iv) Begin to identify, itemize, and design internals-based tests

(3) *Testware deliverables*
- (i)   (Detailed Validation) Test Plans (IEEE/ANSI, 1983 [Std 829-1983])
        – one or more validation activity
- (ii) Verification test plan (for internal design)
- (iii) Verification test report (for internal design)
- (iv) Test design specification (IEEE/ANSI, 1983 [Std 829-1983])

Coding phase

(1) *Inputs to testing*
- (i)   Code (from development)

(2) *Testing tasks*
- (i)   Plan for code verification
- (ii) Analyze the code
- (iii) Verify the code
- (iv) Design externals-based tests
- (v)   Design internals-based tests

(3) *Testware deliverables*
- (i)   Test case specifications (IEEE/ANSI, 1983 [Std 829-1983])
- (ii)   Requirements coverage or tracing matrix
- (iii) Function coverage matrix
- (iv)   Test procedure specifications (IEEE/ANSI, 1983 [Std 829-1983])
- (v)   Verification test plan (for code)
- (vi)   Verification test report (for code)
- (vii) Validation testware (function and system tests)

Integration and test phase

(1) *Inputs to testing*

    (i)   Drafts of user manuals
    (ii) Software to be tested
    (iii) Final user manuals
    (iv) Test item transmittals (IEEE/ANSI, 1983 [Std 829-1983])

(2) *Testing tasks*

    (i)   Planning
    (ii) Review module and integration testing performed by development
    (iii) Perform function tests
    (iv) Perform system tests
    (v) Review draft and final versions of user manuals

(3) *Testware deliverables*

    (i)   Test logs (IEEE/ANSI, 1983 [Std 829-1983])
    (ii) Test incident reports (IEEE/ANSI, 1983 [Std 829-1983])
    (iii) Test summary report (IEEE/ANSI, 1983 [Std 829-1983])

Operation/maintenance phase

(1) *Inputs to testing*

    (i)   (see note)
    (ii) Confirmed problem reports (from any source)

(2) *Testing tasks*

    (i)   Monitor acceptance testing
    (ii) Develop new validation tests for confirmed problems
    (iii) Evaluate continued effectiveness of all tests

(3) *Testware deliverables*

    (i)   Updated test repository

Note: The software life cycle is an iterative process. After the initial release of a product, any change to the product should require that development and testing activities revert to the life-cycle phase that corresponds to the type of change made. For example, if a new function is added to the product (a new function not instigated by a requirements change), then a new functional design specification is required, and the process should revert to the functional design phase and continue sequentially thereafter. In other words, all development and testing activities do not get lumped into the operation/maintenance phase just because the product has been released to customers.

References

IEEE/ANSI (1983). IEEE Standard for Software Test Documentation, (Reaff. 1991), IEEE Std 829-1983.

IEEE/ANSI (1986). IEEE Standard for Software Verification and Validation Plans, (Reaff. 1992), IEEE Std 1012-1986.

IEEE/ANSI (1988). IEEE Standard for Software Review and Audits, IEEE Std 1028-1988.

IEEE/ANSI (1989). IEEE Standard for Software Quality Assurance Plans, IEEE Std 730-1989.

Chapter 11

Software testing tools

The use of testing tools can make testing easier, more effective and more productive. It is no coincidence that one of the first stated goals of attendees at testing courses is: What tools should we buy for my organization?

A wide variety of computer-aided software testing (CAST) tools are available, addressing many aspects of the testing process. Their scope and quality vary widely, and they provide varying degrees of assistance.

If we are to benefit from one of the major sources of leverage in the testing effort, a strategy for evaluation, acquisition, training, implementation, and maintenance is essential. It is an area where independent expertise can be enormously beneficial.

Categorizing test tools

There are a number of ways to categorize testing tools:

(1) *by the testing activity or task in which it is employed* – activities in this case include code verification, test planning, test execution;
(2) *by descriptive functional keyword* – the specific function performed by the tool such as capture/playback, logic coverage, comparator;
(3) *by major areas of classification* – a small number of high-level classes or groupings of tools.

Each class contains tools that are similar in function or other characteristics. Examples of these are test management tools, static analysis tools, and simulators.

The present chapter will focus on the activities with which the tool is associated, namely:

• reviews and inspections
• test planning

- test design and development
- test execution and evaluation
- test support.

We have chosen this approach of categorization for two reasons. First, it is closest to the point of view of the tester – what the tester is doing and when. Second, it is consistent with and based on the testing standards.

A listing of specific tools by descriptive function is included in Appendix G. In general, at the front end of the testing process there are fewer specialized tools available than at the back end.

Tools for reviews and inspections

Tools for reviews and inspections are the tools that assist with performing reviews, walkthroughs, and inspections of requirements, functional design, internal design, and code. Some tools are designed to work with specifications but there are far more tools available that work exclusively with code.

The types of tools required are:

- complexity analysis
- code comprehension
- syntax and semantic analysis.

Complexity analysis
Experienced programmers know that 20% of the code will cause 80% of the problems, and complexity analysis helps to find that all-important 20%. The McCabe Complexity Metrics were originally published in 1982 in the NBS (National Bureau of Standards) publication, "Structured Testing: A Software Testing Methodology Using the Cyclomatic Complexity Metric."

Complexity metrics identify high risk, complex areas. The cyclomatic complexity metric is based on the number of decisions in a program. It is important to testers because it provides an indication of the amount of testing (including inspections) necessary to practically avoid defects. In other words, areas of code identified as more complex are candidates for inspections and additional tests. There are other types of complexity metrics (e.g., from McCabe and Halstead), which in general are an indicator of program testing cost/schedule and number of defects in the program.

Code comprehension
Code comprehension tools help us understand unfamiliar code. They help us to understand dependencies, trace program logic, view graphical representations of the program, and identify dead code. They can be successfully used to identify areas that should receive special attention, such as areas to inspect.

There is a considerable amount of time spent in preparing for a code inspections meeting. This requires extensive analysis, comprehension, and reverse engineering, all of which are made easier by code comprehension tools.

Syntax and semantic analysis

Syntax and semantic analysis tools perform extensive error checking to find errors that a compiler would miss, and are sometimes used to flag potential defects before or sometimes during formal testing.

These tools are language (and sometimes dialect) dependent. With the programming language C, for example, since there are a variety of dialects, these tools can often be configured by dialect. They parse code, maintain a list of errors, and provide build information. The parser can find semantic errors as well as make an inference as to what is syntactically incorrect.

Tools for test planning

The purpose of test planning is to define the scope, approach, resources (including tools), and schedule of testing activities. The test plan provides the foundation for the entire testing process, and, if this sounds like a cerebral activity, it should. Tools don't eliminate the need to think. As useful as capture/playback tools are (see the section on Test execution and evaluation below), they do not replace the need for sound test planning and design.

Perhaps the biggest help here comes from standards. The IEEE/ANSI Standard for Software Test Documentation (Std 829-1983) describes the purpose, outline, and content of the test plan, and the appendix of the standard includes examples taken from commercial data processing. Although a few tools have incorporated templates for test plans into them, many companies have found it useful to simply have someone enter the outline for test plans found in the IEEE/ANSI standard into an accessible edit file.

There are useful commercial tools that determine actual project staffing and schedule needs for adequate product testing. Often people rightly complain that schedules are predetermined by upper management, and the use of such a tool can provide an objective view of the realities of the project.

The types of tools required for test planning are:

- templates for test plan documentation
- test schedule and staffing estimates
- complexity analyzer.

Tools that help with reviews and inspections will also help with test planning, i.e., tools that identify complex product areas can also be used to locate areas that should impact planning for additional tests based on basic risk management.

Tools for test design and development

Test design is the process of detailing the overall test approach specified in the test plan for software features or combinations of features, and identifying and prioritizing the associated test cases. Test development is the process of translating the test design into specific test cases.

Like test planning, there's not a lot of help from test tools for the important, mostly mental process of test design. However, tools from the test execution and evaluation category, for example, capture/playback tools, assist with the development of tests, and are most useful as a means of implementing test cases that have been properly planned and designed.

The types of tools required for test design and development are:

- test data generator
- requirements-based test design tool
- capture/playback
- coverage analysis.

Once again, standards help. The IEEE/ANSI Standard for Software Test Documentation (Std 829-1983) describes the purpose, outline, and content of the test design specification, and the appendix of the standard also includes examples taken from commercial data processing.

Although a few tools have incorporated templates for the test design specification into them, many companies have found it useful to simply have someone enter the outline for test design specifications found in the IEEE/ANSI standard into an accessible edit file.

A useful type of tool in this category is a test data generation tool, which automates the generation of test data based on a user-defined format, for example, automatically generating all permutations of a specific, user-specified input transaction.

A tool that has not yet achieved widespread practical use is a requirements-based test design tool. Based on the assumption that faulty requirements can account for over 80% of the cost of errors, this highly disciplined approach based on cause-effect graph theory is used to design test cases to ensure that the implemented system meets the formally specified requirements document. This approach is for those who desire a disciplined, methodical, rigorous approach.

Test execution and evaluation tools

Test execution and evaluation is the process of executing test cases and evaluating the results. This includes selecting test cases for execution, setting up the environment, running the selected tests, recording the execution activities, analyzing potential product failures, and measuring the effectiveness of the effort. Tools in the evaluation category assist with the process of executing test cases and evaluating the results.

The types of tools required for test execution and evaluation are:

- capture/playback
- coverage analysis
- memory testing
- simulators and performance.

Capture/playback

There is perhaps no chore more boring to the experienced tester than having to repeatedly re-run manual tests. Testers turn to capture/playback tools to automate the execution of tests, in other words, to run tests unattended for hours, overnight, or 24 hours a day if desired.

Capture/playback tools capture user operations including keystrokes, mouse activity, and display output. These captured tests, including the output that has been validated by the tester, form a baseline for future testing of product changes. The tool can then automatically play back the previously captured tests whenever needed and validate the results by comparing them to the previously saved baseline. This frees the tester from having to manually re-run tests over and over again when defect fixes and enhancements change the product.

Capture/playback tools can be classified as either native or non-intrusive. The native (sometimes called intrusive) form of capture/playback is performed within a single system. Both the capture/playback tool and the software being tested reside in the same system, i.e., the test tool is "native" to the system under test. It is sometimes called intrusive because the capture/playback software is distorting the operating performance to some extent, though for most software testing, this distortion is irrelevant.

The non-intrusive form of capture/playback requires an additional hardware system for the test tool. Usually the host system (containing the software under test) has a special hardware connection to the capture/playback tool, and this enables the capture/playback system to perform its required functions transparently to the host software. The best non-intrusive tools are platform and operating system independent.

There are three forms of capture/playback, listed in order of least to most expensive:

(1) *native/software intrusive* (introduces distortion at software level within the system under test);
(2) *native/hardware intrusive* (introduces distortion at hardware level only);
(3) *non-intrusive* (no distortion).

The most common type in use is native/software intrusive. Non-intrusive is typically used when the product being tested is itself an integrated hardware and software system where the introduction of additional internal hardware or software cannot be tolerated, e.g., real-time embedded systems. Since most software testing does not have this constraint, native/software intrusive is usually the cost-effective solution used by most organizations.

Choosing the right capture/playback tool turns out to be one of the most important and also most complex decisions an organization must make regarding testing. Unfortunately, capture/playback tool buyers are often forced to worry about such things as GUI test synchronization, proprietary testing languages, variable execution speed control, portability, multitasking testing, client/server, non-compare filtering, and non-intrusive testing. The best tools combine functionality with ease of use and mask many of the complexities of the tool's internal operation.

Coverage analysis

Coverage analyzers provide a quantitative measure of the quality of tests. In other words, they are a way to find out if the software is being thoroughly tested. This tool, essential to all software test organizations, tells us which parts of the product under test have in fact been executed (covered) by our current tests. They will tell us specifically what parts of the software product are not being covered, and therefore require more tests.

Some companies argue that it is not necessary to achieve full statement coverage, that is, to execute all of the statements within the product prior to release. They seem to think it is all right to expect customers to be the first to execute their code for them. Maybe these companies belong in another line of work. If we aren't measuring coverage, we do not have a handle on the job we are doing as testers.

Almost all structural tools run the source code into a preprocessor so that it can keep track of the coverage information. The problem is we now have a new source that's bigger than the old one so our object module is going to grow in size. The other possible problem is that performance may be impacted because we now have a different program than we did before. However, the final version of the software as delivered does not include the above preprocessing step, and therefore does not suffer this size and performance penalty.

There are many varieties of coverage, including statement, decision, condition, decision/condition, multiple condition, and path. As a minimum, the place to start is to make sure each statement in the program has been tested, and that each decision has taken on all possible outcomes at least once.

Memory testing

Whether being called bounds-checkers, memory testers, run-time error detectors, or leak detectors, in general the tools in this category include the ability to detect:

- memory problems
- overwriting and/or overreading array bounds
- memory allocated but not freed
- reading and using uninitialized memory.

Errors can be identified before they become evident in production and can cause serious problems. Detailed diagnostic messages are provided to allow errors to be tracked and eliminated.

Although memory testing tools tend to be language and platform specific, there are several vendors producing tools for the most popular environments. The top tools in this category are non-intrusive, easy to use, and reasonably priced. We put them in the "Just Do It" category, especially considering the alternative, i.e., shipping low-quality applications.

Test case management

The need for a test case management tool can creep up on us. We begin using a capture/playback tool to build and automate our tests. Then one day we wake up and find we have thousands of disorganized tests that need to be managed.

The best test case managers:

- provide a user interface for managing tests;
- organize tests for ease of use and maintenance;
- start and manage test execution sessions that run user-selected tests;
- provide seamless integration with capture/playback and coverage analysis tools;
- provide automated test reporting and documentation.

Why is test case management in a separate category, i.e., why isn't this incorporated into existing capture/playback tools? The bad news is – we're not there yet. The good news is that several of the leading tool vendors claim that they are working hard to accomplish this, and within the next year or so we should see several viable offerings.

Simulators and performance

Simulators take the place of software or hardware that interacts with the software to be tested. Sometimes they are the only practical method available for certain tests; for instance, when software interfaces with uncontrollable or unavailable hardware devices. They are frequently used to test telecommunications application programs, communications access methods, control programs, and networks.

Simulators also allow us to examine system performance. In general, performance tools help to determine what the software and system performance capabilities are. In practice, it is sometimes hard to find the line that distinguishes a simulator from a performance tool.

Finally, there are tools available for automated multi-user client/server load testing and performance measurement. These tools make it possible to create, control, and analyze the performance testing of client/server applications – before these applications go on line.

Software testing support tools

The test support category includes tools that, while not at the heart of the test process, lend overall support to the overall test effort. When these tools are of poor quality or do not exist, the professional tester suffers.

The types of tools required for test support are:

- problem management
- configuration management.

Problem management

Problem management tools are sometimes called defect tracking tools, bug management tools, incident control systems, etc., and are used to record, track, and generally assist with the management of defects and enhancements throughout the life cycle of software products.

Although many companies spend large sums developing home-grown problem management systems, there are tool vendors who now specialize in creating such systems across a variety of platforms. The best problem management tools are easy to customize for particular environments, and offer as standard features the capability to easily:

- and quickly submit and update defect reports;
- generate pre-defined or user-defined management reports;
- selectively notify users automatically of changes in defect status;
- provide secured access to all data via user-defined queries.

Configuration management

Configuration management (CM) is the key to managing, controlling, and coordinating changes to documents, and whatever else we really care about. CM tools assist the version control and build management process (see Chapter 6).

Besides problem management and configuration management, there are many tools not related to testing that in one way or another support the test process. These include project management tools, data base management software, spreadsheet software, and word processors.

Tool acquisition

The issues to be addressed in the acquisition of tools are largely good management common sense, but they are notoriously hard to implement. Far too often tools are purchased on an *ad hoc*, solve-the-short-term-crisis basis, and as a consequence end up on the shelf gathering dust and regarded as one more expensive experiment.

Making decisions about the acquisition of tools should involve some form of cost/benefit analysis, however simple. Tool vendors are naturally eager to tell us what their tool will do, and how it will solve our particular problems. The question we have to ask is: "At what cost?"

The important thing about cost is to establish true cost – meaning total cost or even lifetime cost. This will be a guesstimate, but it's a lot better than nothing, and as usual the purchase or license price is only the beginning. Additional costs are incurred in selection, installation, operation, training, maintenance and support, and the general cost of reorganizing procedures.

Tools that support testing processes which are already in place can be implemented with much less pain, human and financial, than those which will require an organizational clean sweep.

The scope of initial use needs to be established. Should the new tool be started with a single group, or even selected individuals, or should it be implemented organization-wide immediately?

Management support at the early stages is critical to ensure that the people who are actually working with the new tool can focus their attention on getting up and running and being productive as early as possible.

The careful choice and implementation of tools that support each other and have a synergistic effect is another major source of productivity.

The difficulty is finding the right tools from the right vendors. It is a major undertaking to produce and maintain a current evaluation of available

---

Questions before tool acquisition

There are a few questions that we recommend you answer as part of implementing an effective tools program:

- How do the tools fit into and support our test process?
- Do we know how to plan and design tests? (Tools do not eliminate your need to think, to plan, to design.)
- Who will be responsible for making sure we get the proper training on our new tool?
- Who will promote and support tool use within the organization on an ongoing basis?

testing tools and their capabilities. There are several hundred testing tools on the market, from companies that vary widely in size, installed customer base, product maturity, management depth, and understanding of testing and tools.

For more detail on tools and the tool vendor selection process, see Appendix G.

Independent expert advice at the early stages, preferably from the stage of evaluating processes and deciding what kinds of tools would be useful right up to the implementation stage, is invaluable. There is no doubt that testing can be easier, more effective, and more productive by using tools. By taking the proper steps, we can prevent an expensive new tool from becoming shelfware.

Reference

IEEE/ANSI (1983). IEEE Standard for Software Test Documentation, (Reaff. 1991), IEEE Std 829-1983.

Chapter 12
Measurement

There are a number of big questions for testing – questions about product quality, risk management, release criteria, the effectiveness of the testing process, and when to stop testing.

Measurement provides answers. But once we start to think about what can be measured, it's easy to be overwhelmed with the fact that we could measure almost anything. However, this isn't practical (for the same reason that we can't test everything), and we have to create priorities for measurement based on what measures are critical and will actually be used once we have them.

> "Not everything that counts can be counted, and not everything that can be counted counts."
>
> Albert Einstein

Measurement for the sake of measurement can result in wasted effort. We should ask: "Is it useful? How will we profit from this measure? Is there an important question we could answer satisfactorily if we had reliable measurements in a particular area?" Or perhaps there is an important question we can't ask until we have a particular measurement.

Measurement provides answers

If our planning and subsequent activities are to be effective, they must be developed on a reliable, factual basis. How long should the testing take? How efficient is our testing? How good is our test library? Is it worth doing verification as opposed to validation? How thorough is our validation testing?

Based on past experience, what sort of state is the product likely to be in when it is declared "ready for testing?" What kinds of errors are we likely to find, how many, and where? How many errors probably remain in the product after testing? How is the product doing in test and production compared to other products on the market?

Measuring the number and types of errors detected during verification provides a measure of the efficiency of verification. Verification is expensive, and while we may be convinced that it is cost effective, this effectiveness will often need to be justified to others. How many errors are we picking up in validation that could have been found in verification?

Measuring validation test coverage (requirements, function, and logic coverage) provides quantitative assessments of the thoroughness and comprehensiveness of the validation tests. How much of the product are we testing? How good is our test library?

Measuring/tracking test execution status shows the convergence of key test categories (planned, available, executed, passed) and provides quantitative information on when to stop testing. How many of our tests are planned? How many are available? How many have been executed? How many have passed? When can we (reasonably) stop?

Program complexity provides answers useful when planning the size of the test effort and estimating the number of errors before testing begins.

Measuring and tracking of incident reports (by severity category) is a leading indicator of product quality. It provides an objective criteria for release readiness, a predictor of the number of remaining errors, and generally correlates to users' satisfaction with the product. When normalized, it provides a measure of product quality relative to other products.

When incident reports are not tracked, companies lose the handle on being able to fix problems responsibly. The backlog of incidents grows until it is so large that they no longer have a plan for managing it or getting it down to a reasonable size. Measurement provides an early warning that this situation is developing.

Customer-reported versus testing-reported incidents (only those diagnosed as confirmed errors) provide another measure of testing effectiveness. It is also important that testers have access to defects found by customers because these are a valuable basis for improving the test library (see Hetzel, 1993).

Useful measures

Measuring complexity

Generally, the more complex components of a program are likely to have more errors, and the more focused the testing effort must be to find them. There are plenty of good tools available off the shelf in this area, and it isn't necessary to understand exactly how these tools work to use them efficiently.

There are several well-known measures of program complexity. Most complexity measures can only be calculated after the program is written. Such measures are useful for certain validation tasks and defect prediction.

A simple measure of complexity that is fundamentally a measure of size is lines of code (LOC) or number of source statements, and can be counted in several different ways. A given line might be blank, a comment, one or more executable statements and/or data declarations. Also, there is the problem of comparing the LOC of programs written in different source languages. The simplest way to normalize the LOC is to generate the assembly-language equivalent program and then count LOC. We must decide how to count LOC and then standardize it within the organization. It is less critical to spend an inordinate amount of time debating exactly how to count than it is to count everything exactly the same way using the same tool.

An alternative to counting lines of code is function points. Like lines of code, function points are also a measure of size, effort, and complexity. Unlike lines of code, function points are derived from the user's perspective as detailed in functional specifications, and will stay constant independent of programming language. From the testing process perspective, function points have been used to estimate test cases required per function point and in measuring defects per function point.

In practice, debating lines of code versus function points often becomes a heated, religious discussion. Those that love function points see lines of code as the old, inaccurate approach with many significant shortcomings. The complaints about function points are that they are too abstract, do not relate as closely to what software developers actually produce, require training to learn how to count, and involve a process that seems complex to use to the uninitiated.

Both lines of code and function points today still have a place in software production and are worth considering. In the long term, as function points or a derivative become easy to understand, count, and use, they are likely to eventually completely replace the need to measure lines of code.

Another measure of complexity is McCabe's complexity metric which is the number of decisions (+1) in a program. An N-way branch is equivalent to N–1 decisions. Complexity across subprograms is additive. The result is a complexity number, which if it is above a certain limit, indicates the need for special attention, such as inspections or additional validation testing. Many of the leading tools provide an automatic capability for calculating the McCabe complexity metric.

Halstead's metrics are used for calculating program length (not to be confused with lines of code). Program length can be predicted before the program is written, and the predicted and actual values compare very closely over a wide range of programs. There are also formulas for predicting the number of bugs, programming effort, and time.

Measuring verification efficiency

The efficiency of verification activities is an important measure because verification is expensive. Verification test reports should contain lists of specific errors detected by each verification activity (see Chapter 10). Using subsequent error data from validation activities, one can count the errors detected and the errors missed (not detected) by verification.

Measuring test coverage

Coverage for requirements-based and function-based tests can be measured manually, using a requirements coverage/tracing matrix and a function coverage matrix. Logic coverage can be measured (practically) only with an automated tool. Measuring statement coverage is the most common practice in today's off-the-shelf coverage tools, and in general is a reasonable place to start.

Measuring/tracking test execution status

Test execution tracking is performed most simply by using a spreadsheet. The columns consist of a time stamp and the four test categories: planned, available, executed, passed. Each row is a periodic (e.g., weekly, daily) observation of the number of test cases in each category. The time between successive observations should be small enough to provide a sufficient number of observations to make any trends visible. The spreadsheet can be presented automatically in graphic form to make trends easier to interpret. A predetermined ratio of tests passed to tests planned (e.g., 98%) is often used as one criterion for release.

Measuring/tracking incident reports

Incident or "bug" reports can provide the basis of many valuable quality metrics for software. To realize the full potential of incident reports, the incident reporting process and its automated support system should follow a number of principles:

(1) There should be one and only one way to report an incident. Redundant reporting mechanisms create unnecessary work.

(2) There is a single, master repository for all incident reports. Fragmented, redundant, or incomplete data make it very difficult to obtain accurate, complete, and timely information.

(3) Every incident should be reported via the formal mechanism. Unreported incidents are never investigated. Informal reports often fall through the cracks, and their status cannot be tracked.

(4) Incident reports must rigorously identify the software configuration in which the incident occurred. Users must be able to dynamically obtain from the running system all necessary version information. Version identification can be trusted when it is obtained from the running system.

(5) Every user of a product, not just customers, should take the time to report incidents. This includes internal users, developers, testers, and administrators.

(6) After a new version of a product is baselined for formal testing and potential release (during the integration and test phase), all subsequent incidents should be formally reported. Problems detected before release are just as important as those detected after release.

(7) Every incident report should be investigated and then classified as one of the following:

(i)   user/operator error
(ii)   cannot reproduce the reported problem
(iii) insufficient information
(iv)   documentation (user manual) error
(v)   request for change/enhancement
(vi)   confirmed product error
(vii) other.

(8) Because a raw incident report describes the symptom of a problem (i.e., how the problem manifests itself to the user), the report must contain sufficient space for, or point to, the precise description of the real error. Many quality metrics are based on counts of confirmed errors, not incident reports. It must be possible to count the confirmed errors, not the symptoms of errors, in a specific product. This is not necessarily the product identified in the incident report. Multiple incident reports, each possibly describing different symptoms, should be able to point to the same underlying error without requiring a redundant description of the error in each incident report.

(9) For a confirmed problem, the report must also contain sufficient space for (or point to) the root cause categorization of the error. The best software engineering organizations have cultivated a culture within which a root cause analysis is performed for every confirmed error and then used in error prevention programs. Root causes are often rigorously categorized into a spectrum of standard causes.

(10) The incident reporting system should provide complete tracking information, from the time the report originates to the time it is formally closed. To manage the process, a state transition diagram should be developed to show all possible states of an incident report, the events which cause state changes, and the organizations authorized to make state changes.

(11) An incident report should not be considered closed until all work associated with the report is completed. In the case of a confirmed error, the correction should be available for customer use before the report is closed.

Test measures based on incident reports

The number of confirmed errors per 1,000 lines of code (errors/KLOC) is a common measure of error density that provides one indicator of product quality (or alternatively, the number of confirmed errors per function point). It is also an inter-product comparison of quality. The number of confirmed errors to date is itself a predictor of the number of remaining errors, because the number of undiscovered errors in a program is directly proportional to the number of errors already discovered.

A key component of release criteria usually states the number of confirmed, uncorrected errors (per severity level) that constitutes the limits of acceptability for release to customers. Comparing the number of confirmed errors reported by users and customers to the number reported by testing provides a measure of testing efficiency. The errors reported by users/customers also provide a basis for new test cases.

Other interesting measures

There are many measures of interest to software practitioners. A few of the common ones are:

(1) the age of a detected error;
(2) the response time to fix a reported problem;
(3) the percentage and frequency of detected errors by root-cause category;
(4) error removal efficiency;
(5) error cost:
    (i) cost of the failure to the user
    (ii) cost to investigate and diagnose
    (iii) cost to fix
    (iv) cost to retest
    (v) cost to release.

Recommendations

- Obtain consensus on the top three testing measurements to put in place in your organization.
- Put in place a capability for measuring/tracking test execution status based on the key test status model (planned, available, executed, passed).

- Locate a tool for measuring program complexity.
- Define the testing-related key release criteria and determine how to obtain the measurements.

References

Beizer, B. (1990). *Software Testing Techniques*. Van Nostrand Reinhold.

Capers Jones. (1991). *Applied Software Measurement*. McGraw-Hill.

Hetzel, W. (1993). *Making Software Measurement Work*. QED Publishing Group.

Humphrey, W.S. (1984). *Managing the Software Process*. Reading, MA: Addison-Wesley.

Kit, E. (1986a). *Testing C Compilers*, Computer Standards Conference.

Kit, E. (1986b). *State of the Art, C Compiler Testing*. Tandem Computers Technical Report.

IEEE/ANSI (1988a). IEEE Standard Dictionary of Measures to Produce Reliable Software, IEEE Std 982.1-1988.

IEEE/ANSI (1988b). IEEE Guide for the Use of IEEE Standard Dictionary of Measures to Produce Reliable Software, IEEE Std 982.2-1988.

PART IV

Managing test technology

"Losing the test technology game is losing the software quality game which means losing the software game. Losing the software game is losing the computer game which is losing the high-tech game which in turn means losing the whole post-industrial society ball of wax."

BORIS BEIZER, Losing it, An Essay on World Class Competition

Chapter 13
Organizational approaches to testing

Chapter 14
Current practices, trends, challenges

Chapter 15
Getting sustainable gains in place

Chapter 13
Organizational approaches to testing

Most of us live our lives in organizations that change routinely. We live in structures that are never completely finished. Software testing in particular is an area where companies try many different approaches to organization – partly because of the perplexity about which structures are most effective, i.e., lead to most effective relations between people.

Why do organizations exist? What are the most fundamental, basic building blocks of structural design? What are the advantages and disadvantages of the specific approaches used in the real world to organize software testing? How can we decide which approach to use at this stage of our company?

Organizations exist because there is a need for people as a group to behave predictably and reliably. To achieve results, people need to cooperate with each other. Organizations are created to support, and more to the point, coerce the activities people engage in. Good organizations minimize the inevitable conflict between the needs of the organization and the needs of the individual.

For example, some software organizations have successfully created a positive culture that encourages and rewards migration of individuals from product development groups into independent test development groups equally as much as migration from test to development. In fact, the best cultures reward those who over time complete the full loop – start by spending a few years in development, then spend a few years in test, then return to development.

We have known a few exceptional people to repeat this entire loop twice over a span of about 10 years. The amazing thing is that these people are viewed as the most valued, the most prized resource by managers in both product development and test development. Talk about job security! Why? What better person to have in development than someone who knows how to design a test library? This developer will know how to create software that passes tests, because he or she knows how to think like a tester. And what better person to have designing tests than someone who knows how developers think?

There are many managers who unfortunately only see testing as a training ground for development, not a place to put their best developers. Too bad. I count myself among the managers who *will not hire* a person to do testing unless that person is qualified today to join the development group responsible for developing the same product that he or she would be testing. The good testing manager will encourage such a person to get a few years' experience in product development, and only then to consider moving to the testing group. Radical thinking? We don't think so!

Organizing and reorganizing testing

Once we have personally experienced several reorganizations, we learn to appreciate the need for organizational change to be very carefully planned. Let's face it – organizational change creates stress, disruption, demoralization, and confusion to varying degrees. The following 2200-year old quotation helps us to see how long the problems surrounding organizational change have been recognized and articulated:

> "We trained hard ... but it seemed that every time we were beginning to form up into teams we would be reorganized ... I was to learn later in life that we meet any new situation by reorganizing, and a wonderful method it can be for creating the illusion of progress while producing confusion, inefficiency, and demoralization."
>
> Petronius Arbiter, 210 BC

Isn't it frightening how relevant this thought from Petronius remains today?

An organization is a system that combines materials, knowledge, and methods in order to transform various kinds of inputs into valued outputs. Organizational structure is the responsibilities, authorities, and relationships, arranged in a pattern, through which the organization performs its functions. Structural choices include reporting hierarchies, job descriptions, and goals.

A test organization (usually called a test group) is a resource or set of resources dedicated to performing testing activities. As shops grow, the need for a dedicated, independent testing function becomes a more apparent necessity. It takes unbiased people to produce an unbiased measurement – testing must be done independently if it is to be fully effective in measuring software quality.

Organizational structures are like software. Neither are ever really completely finished. With time, the demands (external and internal) on the structure change – the capability of the existing structure to meet these demands decreases – making organizational redesign a repetitive activity. Likewise, with time, the requirements for a software system change. As with organizations, no matter how well it is designed at the beginning, eventually, if it is to remain useful, software must evolve. *We must leave behind the innocent delusion that once we understand the problem the software system is supposed to solve, we can go off alone to build and test it in peace.*

Test management is difficult. The manager of the test group must have the:

- ability to understand and evaluate software test process, standards, policies, tools, training, and measures;
- ability to maintain a test organization that is strong, independent, formal, and unbiased;
- ability to recruit and retain outstanding test professionals;
- ability to lead, communicate, support, and control;
- time to provide the care needed to manage test groups.

Senior managers must also have the ability to recruit and retain outstanding test managers. In fact, this is usually where the big mistakes are made. The senior managers do not understand the list above enough to know how to evaluate a potential test manager against these requirements. The result is that the wrong person is often promoted into test management!

When making organizational changes that affect testing, senior management needs to understand the impact the change will have on test management's ability to meet the above requirements. Plenty can go wrong when reorganizations occur without sufficient thought being given to the impact on testing. The dangers of having the wrong software testing structure include the following:

- Test independence, formality, and bias is weakened or eliminated.
- People in testing do not participate in reward programs.
- Testing becomes understaffed.
- Testing becomes improperly staffed with too many junior individuals.
- Testing is managed by far too junior managers.
- There is no leverage of test knowledge, training, tools, and process.
- Testing lacks the ability to stop the shipment of poor quality products.
- There is a lack of focused continuous improvement.
- Management lacks the bandwidth to manage testing groups.
- The quality focus is not emphasized.
- Test managers become demoralized owing to lack of career growth.

The above list can be used as a checklist of items to consider when planning organizational modifications. They can become questions; for example: Does making this change weaken the independence of testing? Does it hurt test's ability to get quality resources? etc.

Structural design elements

There is a surprisingly short list of basic building elements from which to construct a structure. The structural design elements are:

(1) *Tall or flat* – There may be many levels between the chief executive officer and the person on the shipping floor (this would be a tall organization), or there might be very few levels (a flat organization). In the last decade, flat has become more popular; managers finding themselves in the middle of a tall organization are particularly vulnerable to losing their jobs.

(2) *Market or product* – The organization may be structured to serve different markets or different products.

(3) *Centralized or decentralized* – The organization may be centralized or decentralized. This is a key question for the test organization. We will examine this in depth later in this chapter.

(4) *Hierarchical or diffused* – The organization may be hierarchical, that is, organized according to successively higher levels of authority and rank. Or it may be diffused, which is widely spread or scattered or matrixed.

(5) *Line or staff* – The organization will have a certain mix of line and/or staff roles.

(6) *Functional or project* – The organization may have functional or project orientations.

Combining these few design elements provides quite a variety of operating structural designs. Sometimes a variety of designs are implemented within the same company.

Approaches to organizing the test function

The above organizational basic design elements can be combined to produce many different test structures. There are seven approaches to organizing testing typically taken in practice that reflect the evolution of a maturing development organization. The following approaches to structure assume that unit testing should be done by product development. Therefore, the material that follows is about testing activities not related to unit testing, e.g., function testing, system testing, etc.

Approach 1. Testing is each person's responsibility

Approach 1 is what often occurs in the real world, especially when companies are small and little thought has been given to testing. As shown in Figure 13.1, there is a group of product developers whose primary responsibility is to

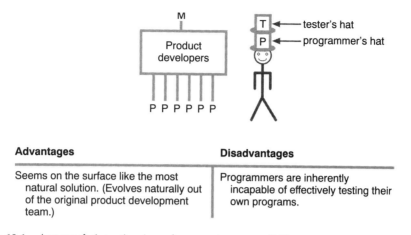

Advantages	Disadvantages
Seems on the surface like the most natural solution. (Evolves naturally out of the original product development team.)	Programmers are inherently incapable of effectively testing their own programs.

Figure 13.1   Approach 1: testing is each person's responsibility.

build a product. In this model, these product developers also are responsible for testing their own code. These people unfortunately must try their best to wear two hats, a programmer's hat and a tester's hat. They are responsible for function testing, system testing, and any other kind of testing that gets done.

The problem with this approach is that it violates a basic assumption. Testing must be done independently if it is to be fully effective in measuring software quality. Programmers are biased by the creative work they do. This blinds them to their own errors; it is human nature.

Approach 2. Testing is each unit's responsibility

Approach 2 fixes the obvious flaw encountered in approach 1 – that of programmers being inherently incapable of testing their own programs – by assigning product developers within the group the job of testing each other's code. Note from Figure 13.2 that each person is still wearing two hats: the person on the right is responsible for product development of their own modules, plus they must test their team-mate's modules.

The problem now is for these people to find the time to understand the job of the software testing professional as well as understand product development processes, standards, policies, tools, training, metrics, etc. For typical software industry projects, this is just asking too much of one person. It is like expecting your average construction site hire to be a master electrician and a master carpenter on the same project at the same time. It is not impossible, it can occur – it is just not likely and does not make much sense.

In reality, these people will pick one hat to wear – the hat for which they know they have the primary responsibility and for which they are evaluated by management – the hat of the product developer. They will take time to test other people's code as time and skills permit. They will usually not get very good at learning the special skills, tools, and methods of testing while they are simultaneously responsible for developing product. That's reality.

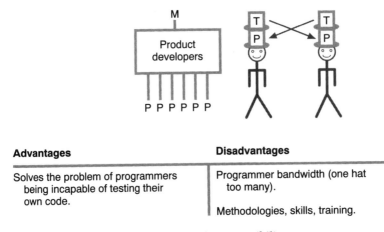

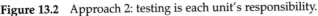

Advantages	Disadvantages
Solves the problem of programmers being incapable of testing their own code.	Programmer bandwidth (one hat too many).
	Methodologies, skills, training.

Figure 13.2 Approach 2: testing is each unit's responsibility.

Approach 3. Testing is performed by dedicated resource

Approach 3 solves the developer bandwidth issue by selecting a product developer and giving them a new job, that of test developer. Note from Figure 13.3 that each person in the group now only has to wear one professional hat. The tricky part here is for the group manager to pick the right person for testing.

In the evolutionary beginning, we noted that there was no test organization at all. One day the manager wakes up and declares, "All right, I see, I believe now. I know we need a dedicated person for testing. Hmmm, whom shall I tap to be our tester?" This really happens. Once while the author was presenting a course on testing, a development manager raised his hand and

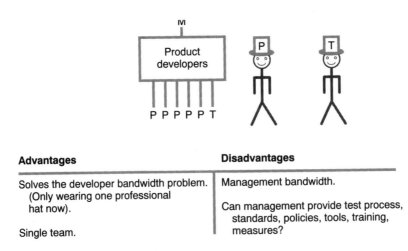

Advantages	Disadvantages
Solves the developer bandwidth problem. (Only wearing one professional hat now).	Management bandwidth.
Single team.	Can management provide test process, standards, policies, tools, training, measures?

Figure 13.3 Approach 3: Testing performed by dedicated resource.

stated, "OK, OK, now I understand what testing is all about. I'm going to put our first full-time independent tester in place!" Great, thinks the course instructor, feeling very good about his teaching abilities.

"Yea", the manager continues, "I have this person that just doesn't fit on the development team. They've been a consistently poor performer; they're unhappy and they are just not contributing anything to reaching our project goals. I was going to fire them, but that is such an unpleasant task for me. I'll make them a tester! What have I got to lose?"

Of course we know he's got plenty to lose. The individual wearing too many hats now is the first line product development manager. This person, in addition to providing guidance to a product development team, must provide guidance on testing process, testing standards, testing policies, testing tools, testing training, testing measures, hiring professional testers, etc. It is just not going to happen.

It becomes clear that some sort of test group is necessary – a set of resources dedicated to performing testing activities and managed by a test manager. Without a formal organization, testing practices and tools must be set up for every project. With a separate test group, however, an organization remains in place to serve all projects on a continuing basis – to provide management with independent, unbiased, quality information.

Bill Hetzel, in the book *The Complete Guide to Software Testing* (1988), tells us:

> An independent test organization is important because
> * building systems without one has not worked well,
> * effective measurement is essential to product quality control,
> * coordinating testing requires full-time, dedicated effort.

The creation of a formal test organization solves the problem of approach 3. Note in Figure 13.4 the importance of a test organization is realized, headed by a test manager. The question now becomes where to put the test group organizationally.

Approach 4. The test organization in QA

A common solution is to make the new test organization a component of quality assurance, where QA also audits the development process (see Figure 13.5). The manager of QA may not understand software testing. The capabilities of management of the testing group are critical, as is the manager of the testing manager. Since testing is performed in a separate organization from development, it will take extra effort to encourage and create a positive team environment. People also begin to ask, who owns quality? Development management complains that they no longer have the complete set of resources needed to produce a quality product.

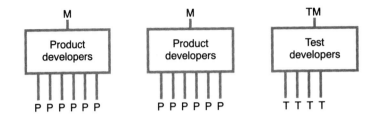

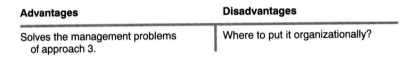

Advantages	Disadvantages
Solves the management problems of approach 3.	Where to put it organizationally?

Figure 13.4   The test organization.

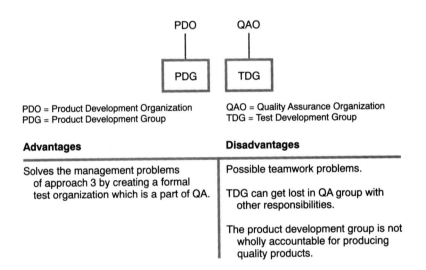

PDO = Product Development Organization
PDG = Product Development Group

QAO = Quality Assurance Organization
TDG = Test Development Group

Advantages	Disadvantages
Solves the management problems of approach 3 by creating a formal test organization which is a part of QA.	Possible teamwork problems. TDG can get lost in QA group with other responsibilities. The product development group is not wholly accountable for producing quality products.

Figure 13.5   Approach 4: the test organization in QA.

Approach 5. The test organization in development

Approach 5 attempts to deal with the teamwork and quality ownership issue identified in approach 4 by creating a test organization that is part of the development organization (see Figure 13.6). This approach usually puts the test group under the second line product development manager.

Unfortunately, this is asking too much of most second line product development managers. It is much less an issue for higher level managers such as vice presidents that understand the need for a strong, independent

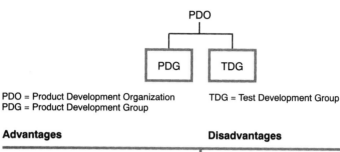

PDO = Product Development Organization   TDG = Test Development Group
PDG = Product Development Group

Advantages	Disadvantages
Solves the management problems of approach 3 by creating a formal test organization which is a part of development. Possibly solves teamwork issues of approach 4.	Does the senior development manager meet the test management requirements?

Figure 13.6   Approach 5: the test organization in development.

test function and who are willing to put a strong manager in place to manage the test group. In any event, all is riding on the senior manager who is now the one wearing two hats, that of managing the management responsible for product development and of managing the management responsible for software testing.

As organizations grow, more people are hired into the test organization, and multiple test groups are needed. A new issue arises. Should the multiple test groups be centrally or decentrally organized?

Approach 6. Centralized test organization

Approach 6 solves the senior management problem of approach 5 by creating a central test organization that lives within and serves a product development division (see Figure 13.7). Note how this creates a major opportunity for a senior test manager/director to significantly impact the organization. For example, the senior test manager can:

- manage the sharing of testing resources (both people and equipment) to smooth needs and better manage the risks of the company;
- coordinate consistent training for all testers across several test groups;
- promote consistent and high-quality testing tools for use by all testers;
- find and hire strong first line testing managers;
- provide real testing guidance to first line test managers.

In addition, first line testing managers see a potential career path in testing as they aspire to become a senior test manager.

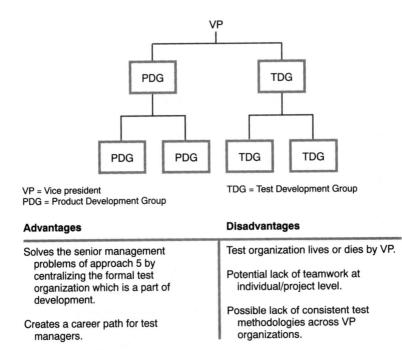

VP = Vice president
PDG = Product Development Group

TDG = Test Development Group

Advantages	Disadvantages
Solves the senior management problems of approach 5 by centralizing the formal test organization which is a part of development. Creates a career path for test managers.	Test organization lives or dies by VP. Potential lack of teamwork at individual/project level. Possible lack of consistent test methodologies across VP organizations.

Figure 13.7   Approach 6: centralized test organization.

Now the risks are centralized, and assuming a good senior test manager is in place, the testing organization will live or die by the vice president who manages the product development and the test development organizations. When it's time to determine headcount, capital, and rewards for software testing, the vice president must provide the crucial support.

With the right vice president, this can and has often worked quite well in practice. A vice president that provides the proper resources, hires well, and delegates well to a highly competent senior test manager can make this approach work extremely well.

By creating project teams that are loaned resources from the independent test organization and that otherwise act, communicate, and live close together as a team alongside the product developers, the previously stated teamwork disadvantages are minimized. And when serious discussions regarding product quality are needed, a senior test manager is there to provide an unbiased voice to the vice president. This can be of great value to a vice president who cannot get the complete set of facts from product development management.

As companies continue to grow larger and contain multiple divisions, companies using this approach may begin to discover a lack of consistent approaches and best practices across different vice president organizations. This is solved by the next and final approach.

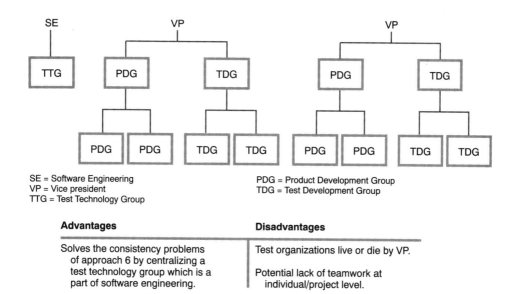

SE = Software Engineering
VP = Vice president
TTG = Test Technology Group

PDG = Product Development Group
TDG = Test Development Group

Advantages	Disadvantages
Solves the consistency problems of approach 6 by centralizing a test technology group which is a part of software engineering.	Test organizations live or die by VP. Potential lack of teamwork at individual/project level.

Figure 13.8   Approach 7: centralized and test technology.

Approach 7. Centralized test organization with a test technology center

Approach 7 solves the consistency problems of approach 6 by creating a test technology group, which in this case is part of a software engineering function (see Figure 13.8). This new test technology group is responsible for:

- leading and managing testing process and testing productivity improvement efforts;
- driving and coordinating testing training programs;
- coordinating the planning and implementation of testing tool programs;
- documenting test process, standards, policies, and guidelines as necessary;
- recognizing and leveraging best practices within the testing groups;
- recommending, obtaining consensus for, and implementing key testing measurements.

Selecting the right approach

How can we decide from among the many different approaches to using these structural design elements? To begin with, below is a set of sample selection criteria that can be used as a basis for evaluating different approaches. To what extent does the organizational structure:

- provide the ability for rapid decision making;
- enhance teamwork, especially between product development and testing development;
- provide for an independent, formal, unbiased, strong, properly staffed and rewarded, test organization;
- help to coordinate the balance of testing and quality responsibilities;
- assist with test management requirements as stated earlier in this chapter;
- provide ownership for test technology;
- leverage the capabilities of available resources, particularly people;
- positively impact morale and career path of employees (including managers)?

Providing for rapid decision making leads to improved responsiveness. It is possible to overcome an organizational structure that does not inherently provide for rapid decision making by creating special core teams and/or defining a special rapid escalation process, i.e., a daily high-level management short decision meeting used to escalate and deal with project issues.

One approach to doing reorganizations is to follow these steps:

(1) map the current organization;
(2) define and prioritize the key selection criteria (see list above);
(3) document new potential alternative approaches;
(4) evaluate potential approaches using a selection grid (see below);
(5) decide on a new organization;
(6) implement the new organization.

A decision matrix selection grid is a quality tool that can be used to evaluate the various approaches while using the selection criteria. Once the selection criteria are decided, they can be numbered or uniquely identified and placed across the top of the decision matrix.

The possible approaches are also numbered and placed vertically on the matrix as shown in Figure 13.9. Each approach is evaluated by considering each selection criteria and assigning a number to enter into the matrix. This number would come from a pre-defined range of values, e.g., from 1 to 5, where 5 indicates a high ranking, meaning the organization to a very great

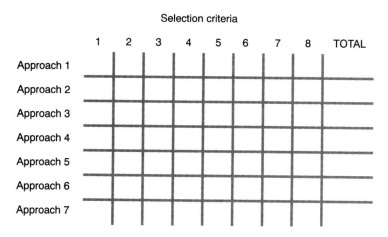

Figure 13.9 Decision matrix selection grid.

extent meets the given criteria for the approach under consideration. Likewise 3 might indicate a medium ranking and 1 a low ranking.

Add the scores horizontally to yield a total score for each approach. As a more advanced enhancement to this approach, the selection criteria can be assigned a multiplier weighting to be factored in.

Reorganizations should be carefully planned and implemented. One last piece of advice – remember to involve the participants in the above process!

References

Beizer, B. (1992). "Losing It, An Essay on World Class Competition," *Software Quality World*, **4**(3).

Goodman, Paul, Sproull & Associates (1990). *Technology and Organizations*. San Francisco, CA: Jossey-Bass.

Gelperin, D. and Hetzel, W. (1989). *STEP: Introduction and Summary Guide*. Jacksonville, FL: Software Quality Engineering.

Hetzel, W. (1988). *The Complete Guide to Software Process*. Wellesley, MA: QED Information Sciences.

Humphrey, W.S. (1989). *Managing the Software Process*. Reading, MA: Addison-Wesley.

Kaner, C. (1988). *Testing Computer Software*. Blue Ridge Summit, PA: TAB Books.

Kit, E. (1992). "Approaches to Organizing the Independent Test Function," *Software Testing Analysis & Review (STAR) Conference Proceedings*.

Silverman, M. (1984). *The Technical Manager's Survival Book*. New York: McGraw-Hill.

Chapter 14

Current practices, trends, challenges

Advances in technology and development tools have enabled the creation of complex software using graphical user interfaces (GUIs) and client/server application architectures. Although these advances have improved development productivity, the resulting software is difficult to test, and the new demands on testing are eroding the development productivity gains achieved. Automation through commercial testing tools is stepping in to fill part of the gap.

During the short history of software engineering, there has been a dramatic shift in tester-to-developer ratios (in favor of the testers) which indicates that the importance of testing is now recognized, and organizations are now more willing to pay for proper testing. At the same time the number of testers continues to grow, and time spent on testing and its perceived effectiveness are increasing.

Meanwhile, studies of best practice in the industry indicate that the strictly non-technical basics – good management, communications, people, and controls – are more important to testing success than state-of-the-art methodologies, CASE tools, and other silver bullets.

GUIs: What's new here ?

There are two types of user interfaces:

(1) character-based user interfaces (traditional style);
(2) GUIs.

GUIs are characterized by the use of a different input device (mouse) and by high-resolution spatial and color images. GUI testing requires increased automation, but this is much more complicated in a GUI environment than a character-based environment. Fortunately, the new generation of capture/replay tools provides the answer (see Chapter 11).

176

Usage testing

Knowing how the product is really going to be used enables us to focus on certain types of critical areas when testing. When we prioritize validation tests, we are already, usually subconsciously, making judgments about potential usage. Usage testing is a more formal approach to this problem.

Usage testing is the process of:

- initial testing based on *estimated* usage patterns;
- measuring (collecting data on) the actual usage (after the product is complete and functional), and developing an *operational profile*;
- adjusting priorities, developing new tests, and retesting, based on the operational profile.

Usage testing reflects expected operational use in hardware and software configurations, in the frequency of operations tested, in the sequence of operations tested and in system load. Testing emphasis is on detecting errors that are the most likely to occur in operational use.

Usage testing is ideally performed after unit and integration testing, when substantial functionality is available, and after requirements validation – if it is performed separately. In practice it is usually performed after developing operational profiles based on real usage by real users, and this may mean that usage testing can apply only to releases after the first.

The advantages of usage testing are that it is customer oriented; test resources and schedules are optimized to maximize customer satisfaction. The hard part is cost-effectively obtaining operational profiles, which is why many companies today are not formally doing usage testing. However, most leading software companies do factor-in known or expected customer usage of the product when prioritizing tests worth developing.

Usage testing was pioneered by Frank Ackerman (1992, 1993), formerly of the Institute for Zero Defect Software.

Tester-to-developer ratios

Tester-to-developer staffing ratios are an interesting indication of the number of people performing testing activities compared to the number of people developing the software product. Ratios have improved dramatically in favor of more testers during the short and stormy life of the software engineering discipline.

Historically, for mainframes, the tester-to-developer ratio was 1:5–10, meaning one tester for every five to ten product developers. More recently published numbers include:

- Microsoft, 1992   2:3
- Lotus (for 1-2-3 Windows)   2:1
- Average of 4 major companies (1992)   1:2

(*Note*: The Microsoft and Lotus reference is Marvin (1993). The Microsoft ratio is for the Microsoft Worldwide Product Division. The four companies referenced are Microsoft, Borland, WordPerfect, and Novell for which the reference is Norman (1993).)

The above figures should be viewed as above average, that is, applying more testers than most companies do in practice. Informal surveys performed during testing courses taught by Software Development Technologies indicate that most companies do not enjoy ratios as good as one testing professional for every two product developers. More typical ratios are in the range from 1:3 to 1:4. Most testing professionals surveyed from companies operating at 1:5 or above (e.g., 1:7, 1:10, or even 1:20) generally felt that testing was under-resourced.

Software measures and practices benchmark study

This important study was a joint initiative by Xerox Corporation and Software Quality Engineering to improve understanding of software excellence. The goal of the study was to identify world-class projects in software technology and to characterize the engineering, management and measurement practices of these projects. A full research report is available from Software Quality Engineering (1991).

The design of the study included two phases. The purpose of phase 1 was to identify the "best" projects. Seventy-five software organizations were surveyed and responded to 52 questions (15 on the organization and 37 on its practices). The purpose of phase 2 was to characterize the practices of the "best" projects. Ten "best" projects (7 companies, 509 people) were surveyed, and responded to 104 questions (17 on attitude, 87 on practices and measures) and were subjected to an on-site practices assessment.

"Best" projects were selected on the following basis:

- perceived as producing high-quality results;
- perceived as using better practices;
- implemented recently or in final test with project team accessible for interview.

In other words, the best practices were reverse engineered from projects identified subjectively as having the highest quality – the projects the organization was the most proud of.

Companies were selected for phase 2 on the following basis:

- software a significant part of organizational mission;
- high scores on Phase 1 survey (above 75th percentile);
- reputation and public perception of success.

The actual phase 2 companies were:

- AT&T
- Dupont
- GTE
- IBM
- NCR
- Siemens
- Xerox.

The key findings of the study were:

(1) best projects emphasize strong up-front planning and close tracking and reporting of status on an ongoing basis;

(2) best projects rely on management fundamentals (teamwork, communication, and controls), not on technology and state-of-the-art methodologies;

(3) best projects emphasize reviews, inspections, and very strong and independent high-level testing;

(4) measurement used to track progress, quality problems, and issues.

(5) seven practices in common use related to planning and up-front requirements and design specifications;

(6) best projects utilized recommended practices – the investment required to achieve a more disciplined and structured process is evident in the results;

(7) best projects excel in different areas (survey categories) and emphasize different phases of the life cycle; no single project was superior in all areas.

The key measurement practices were discovered to be:

- schedule performance

- code defects
- test results
- test defects
- defects after release
- number of open problems
- time to correct problems
- issue tracking
- lines of code
- process compliance.

There are no silver bullets here. The keys to success are basic issues:

- good management
- good communications
- good people
- good controls
- ongoing measurements.

References

Ackerman, F. (1993). "Usage Testing," *Software Testing Analysis & Review (STAR) Conference Proceedings 1992.*

Ackerman, F. (1994). "Constructing and using Operational Profiles," *Software Testing Analysis & Review (STAR) Conference Proceedings 1993.*

Norman, S. (1993). "Testing GUIs is a sticky business," *Software Testing Analysis & Review (STAR) Conference Proceedings 1992.*

Software Quality Engineering (1991) Report 908.

Tener, M. (1993). "Testing in the GUI and Client/Server World," *IBM OS/2 Developer,* Winter.

Chapter 15

Getting sustainable gains in place

Only with a strong commitment to proven software engineering practices can companies successfully compete, survive, and thrive in today's marketplace. The necessary changes and investments to advance the state of the practice must be made; the alternative is to lose everything. Years of consulting experience, corroborated by the Xerox study (see Chapter 14), makes it clear that if we focus on planning, communication, tracking, and measurement, we'll substantially increase our odds of creating products with the right level of quality.

Getting gains to happen

Being an agent for change is hard. Whether you're striving for small or large changes, tactical or strategic improvements, those that require cultural evolution or revolution, take the time to assess the situation and plan for gains that are sustainable. Before proceeding, take a step back, look carefully around you. Are you facing small cracks in the pavement ahead or a deep crevasse? The strategy will be different for each. Taking the recurrent advice of making small steps in the name of continuous improvement when facing a large crevasse can be disastrous! Remember, as the Chinese proverb says:

> "It is very dangerous to try and leap a chasm in two bounds."

Changing an organization is hard. Change must be positive, planned, and controlled, with a minimum of disruption, and a minimum of culture shock. Try to determine the readiness for change: How much pain is the organization feeling now? How much pain are our customers feeling now? What is the internal level of dissatisfaction with the status-quo versus the level of natural resistance to change (Migdoll, 1993)?

The benefits of change have to be defined, and the expected improvements justified. Change has to be sold to managers and practitioners throughout the organization. Measure the effectiveness of changes that have been implemented, and publicize them. People need to feel they are participating in (and paying a price for) something that is working.

Ultimately, management must lead the way. Management suffers the effects of poor practices: receiving letters of complaint from customers, losing a key account, and getting sued. If management can see what's wrong, and can also see what can be done about it, another vital building block for sustained improvement is in place. Management support is vital during the rough patches when enthusiasm fades.

Getting help

The early software testing specialists did not have software engineering standards, testing tools, courses, books, and conferences available to them. But we're not in this alone any more.

Software testing books and newsletters

Sometimes the best place to begin is with a good book. If you can afford to invest in two books, pick one of the current testing books and the classic, *The Art of Software Testing* by Glenford Myers (1979). Then if your company can afford another $50, do the entire organization a favor and buy *Managing the Software Process* by Watts Humphrey (1989), but don't keep it for yourself. Give it to whoever heads software development, because they are in the best position to fix the development process, which in turn will make your life in software testing better. For detailed information on these and other useful books on software engineering and software testing, see the list in Appendix E.

For a list of journals and newsletters for testing managers and practitioners, all of which are invaluable sources of information on practice and general comparisons of experience within the testing community, see Appendix F.

Consulting and training services

The use of external consultants can help instigate change. In an organization fraught with political problems and pressure, an independent consultant can promote a neutral, unbiased viewpoint without political risk. When people are too close to the real problem, a consultant can provide an industry-wide perspective including experiences drawn from many different organizations.

Training provides people at all levels with a sound knowledge of the techniques and concepts they need. Training is a critical measure of the commitment of the organization to invest in developing the expertise of its staff and its determination to stay ahead of the game.

Training and consulting services to improve development processes are available to satisfy customers worldwide. Typically these services are provided directly to software product developers, software test developers, and management. When choosing a provider of training and consulting services, consider using the following assessment list:

- Do they have proven development and testing experience?
- Can they offer proven, practical, effective solutions?
- Can they provide a technology assessment to examine the existing approach to developing and testing software?
- How do they identify and prioritize the areas in greatest need of improvement?
- Do they offer a full range of verification and validation services?
- Do they have a permanent staff of experienced methodologists available to design a custom solution for your needs?
- Do they have instructors who are experienced senior software engineers and managers with excellent technical, communication, and instructional skills?
- Do they have consultants who are experts in software technologies that apply to your type of software?
- Are they prominent technology leaders, authors, conference speakers, and leaders of national software standards efforts?
- Can they provide an extensive list of satisfied customers?

Do not hesitate to ask for biographical information on the instructor or consultant who will be providing services for you. It should include the number of years they have been providing services. (See also Appendix G.)

Software testing conferences

Attendees at software testing conferences include those responsible for test and evaluation activities, including the working practitioner and manager, lead quality assurance specialists, systems analysts, project managers, and programmers. Since many companies tend to send their senior people, the networking opportunities can be very valuable.

In general, the software testing conferences consist of:

(1) Pre-conference tutorials, in which experts focus on selected topics for one half to two days, depending on the conference and the topic. Typical topics include An Overview of Software Testing, Software Inspections, Testing Object Orientated Systems, Client/Server Testing, GUI Testing.

(2) General sessions, in which experts and industry leaders share technical insights and perspectives on trends in the field and offer recommendations to attendees.

(3) A testing tools exhibit which is usually held for one or two days of the conference, normally drawing 20 to 30 vendors. Products and services that support software testing are displayed. Most vendors prepare demonstrations of their latest software testing tools.

(4) Presentation tracks where multiple track sessions run in parallel; attendees select tracks that emphasize practitioner presentations on topics of interest, for example, management, tools, methods, process improvement.

Pricing varies, usually from $300 to $1,500, depending on the conference and whether attendance includes the pre-conference tutorials. Attendance varies also, usually from 200 to 600 people.

For additional information on individual testing conferences see Appendix F.

Follow-up

Implementing improvement is a "forever after" commitment. Don't be afraid to make long-term plans as well as going for the small, steady, perceptible short-term gains that, taken together, make very big differences over time. If you get stuck, go back to the basic premises of this book – and to proven, solid engineering principles.

Someone must be responsible for the overall improvement process – for planning and managing the whole set of improvements – someone who checks with individual improvement process owners regularly to see how they are doing. If no one within the company is available, find a good consultant to fill this role to ensure that you are always going forward. Remember that a prolonged period of no progress means you are going backward relative to others who are getting improvements in place.

How do we know we are are achieving improvement? Find metrics that tell you. Measure something simple like document availability, for instance. If you can make comparisons on a measurable, repeatable basis, you are on the road to proper process control and maturity.

Real progress means sustainable gains – gains that will stay in place when staff change, when development projects and the type of customers being serviced are different from what they are now, and when the inevitable reorganization happens. These gains may be in increments of 5% or less, but improvement, though hard to get started, is compounded, and each step makes the one which follows it easier.

References

Humphrey, W.S. (1989). *Managing the Software Process*. Reading, MA: Addison-Wesley.

Migdoll, M. (1993). "Improving Test Practices," *Software Testing Analysis & Review (STAR) Conference Proceedings*.

Myers, G. (1979). *The Art of Software Testing*. John Wiley.

Appendices

Appendix A
Standards relevant to software engineering and testing

Appendix B
Verification checklists

Appendix C
Verification exercises

Appendix D
Validation exercises (solutions)

Appendix E
Bibliography (includes listing of software testing tools catalogs)

Appendix F
Sources: conferences, journals, newsletters, DOD specifications

Appendix G
Specific tools and tool selection

Appendix H
Sample lists of improvements to be implemented

Appendix A
Standards relevant to software engineering and testing

Key software testing standards

IEEE/ANSI Standard 829-1983
IEEE Standard for Software Test Documentation (Reaff. 1991)
This standard defines the content and format of eight documents that cover the entire testing process. The test plan prescribes the scope, approach, resources, and schedule of the testing activities. It defines the items to be tested, the testing tasks to be performed, the personnel responsible for each task, and the risks associated with the plan. The standard shows the relationship of these documents to one another as they are developed, and to the test process they document.

IEEE/ANSI Standard 1008-1987
IEEE Standard for Software Unit Testing (Reaff. 1993)
Software unit testing is a process that includes the performance of test planning, the development of a test set, and the measurement of a test unit against its requirement. Measuring entails the use of sample data to exercise the unit and the comparison of the unit's actual behavior with its required behavior as specified in the unit's requirement documentation.

This standard defines an integrated approach to systematic and documented unit testing. The approach uses unit design and unit implementation information, in addition to unit requirements, to determine the completeness of the testing. The standard describes a testing process composed of a hierarchy of phases, activities, and tasks. Further, it defines a minimum set of tasks for each activity, although additional tasks may be added to any activity.

Other standards related to software testing

IEEE/ANSI Standard 1012-1986
IEEE Standard for Software Verification and Validation Plans (Reaff. 1992)
This standard has a threefold purpose:

(1) To provide, for both critical and non-critical software, uniform and minimum requirements for the format and content of software verification and validation plans (SVVPs).

(2) To define, for critical software, specific minimum verification and validation (V&V) tasks and their required inputs and outputs that shall be included in SVVPs.

(3) To suggest optional V&V tasks to be used to tailor SVVPs as appropriate for the particular V&V effort.

IEEE/ANSI Standard 1028-1988
IEEE Standard for Software Reviews and Audits
Software reviews and audits are a basic part of the ongoing evaluation of software products as they pass along the software development cycle. This standard provides direction to the reviewer or auditor on the conduct of evaluations. Included are processes applicable to both critical and non-critical software and the procedures required for the execution of reviews and audits.

IEEE/ANSI Standard 730-1989
IEEE Standard for Software Quality Assurance Plans
This standard has legal liability as its basic rationale. It is directed toward the development and maintenance of critical software, that is, where failure could impact safety or cause large financial or social losses. The orientation is toward delineating all of the planned and systematic actions on a particular project that would provide adequate confidence that the software product conforms to established technical requirement.

This standard establishes a required format and a set of minimum contents for software quality assurance plans.

IEEE/ANSI Standard 610.12-1990
Standard Glossary of Software Engineering Terminology
This standard is a revision and redesignation of IEEE Standard 729. This standard contains definitions for more than 1,000 terms, establishing the basic vocabulary of software engineering. Building on a foundation of American National Standards Institute (ANSI) and International Organization for Standardization (ISO) terms, it promotes clarity and consistency in the vocabulary of software engineering and associated fields.

Other software engineering standards

IEEE/ANSI Standard 828-1990
IEEE Standard for Software Configuration Management Plans
This standard is similar in format to IEEE Standard 730, but deals with the more limited subject of software configuration management. The standard identifies requirements for configuration identification, configuration control, configuration status accounting and reporting, and configuration audits and reviews. The implementation of these requirements provides a means by which the evolution of the software product items are recorded, communicated, and controlled. It provides assurance of the integrity and continuity of the software product items as they evolve through the software development and maintenance life cycle.

IEEE/ANSI Standard 830-1993
IEEE Recommended Practice for Software Requirements Specifications
This guide describes alternate approaches to good practice in the specification of software requirements. To enable the reader to make knowledgeable choices, extensive tutorial material is provided. This guide covers the attributes of a good software requirements specification, as well as specification methodologies and associated formats.

IEEE/ANSI Standard 982.1-1988
IEEE Standard Dictionary of Measures to Produce Reliable Software
This standard provides definitions of selected measures. The measures are intended for use throughout the software development life cycle in order to produce reliable software. The standard does not specify or require the use of any of the measures. Its intent is to describe the individual measures and their use.

A companion to this standard, 982.2, provides guidance in the use of the measures in IEEE Standard 982.1. It provides information needed by industry to make the best use of IEEE Standard 982.1.

IEEE/ANSI Standard 990-1987
IEEE Recommended Practice for Ada as a Program Design Language (Reaff. 1992)
This recommended practice provides recommendations reflecting state-of-the-art and alternate approaches to good practice for characteristics of Program Design Languages (PDLs) based on the syntax and semantics of the Ada programming language. In this document, these are referred to as Ada PDLs.

IEEE/ANSI Standard 1002-1987
IEEE Standard Taxonomy for Software Engineering Standards (Reaff. 1992)
This standard describes the form and content of a software engineering standards taxonomy. It explains the various types of software engineering standards, their functional and external relationships, and the role of various functions participating in the software life cycle. The taxonomy may be used as a method for planning the development or evaluation of standards for an organization. It could also serve as a basis for classifying a set of standards or for organizing a standards manual.

IEEE/ANSI Standard 1016-1987
IEEE Recommended Practice for Software Design Descriptions (Reaff. 1993)
A software design description is a representation of a software system. It is used as a medium for communicating software design information. This recommended practice describes that documentation of software designs. It specifies the necessary information content and the recommended organization for a software design description.

IEEE/ANSI Standard 1042-1987
IEEE Guide to Software Configuration Management (Reaff. 1993)
The purpose of this guide is to provide guidance in planning Software Configuration Management (SCM) practices that are compatible with IEEE Standard 828. The guide

focuses on the process of SCM planning and provides a broad perspective for the understanding of software configuration management.

IEEE/ANSI Standard 1045-1992
IEEE Standard for Software Productivity Metrics
This standard defines a framework for measuring and reporting productivity of the software process. It focuses on definitions of how to measure software process productivity and what to report when giving productivity results. It is meant for those who want to measure the productivity of the software process for creating code and documentation products.

IEEE/ANSI Standard 1058.1-1987
IEEE Standard for Software Project Management Plans (Reaff. 1993)
This standard specifies the format and contents of software project management plans. It does not specify the procedures or techniques to be used in the development or project management plans, nor does it provide examples of project management plans. Instead, the standard sets a foundation for an organization to build its own set of practices and procedures for developing project management plans.

IEEE/ANSI Standard 1061-1992
IEEE Standard for a Software Quality Metrics Methodology
This standard provides a methodology for establishing quality requirements and identifying, implementing, analyzing, and validating the process and product of software quality metrics. This standard does not prescribe specific metrics, but does include examples of metrics together with a complete example of the standard's use.

IEEE/ANSI Standard 1063-1987
IEEE Standard for Software User Documentation (Reaff. 1993)
This standard provides minimum requirements on the structure and information content of user documentation. It applies primarily to technical substance rather than to style. Users of this standard may develop their own style manual for use within their organizations to implement the requirements of this standard.

IEEE/ANSI Standard 1074-1991
IEEE Standard for Developing Software Life Cycle Processes
This standard defines the set of activities that constitute the processes that are mandatory for the development and maintenance of software. The management and support processes that continue throughout the entire life cycle, as well as all aspects of the software life cycle from concept exploration through retirement, are covered. Associated input and output information is also provided. Utilization of the processes and their component activities maximizes the benefits to the user when using this standard life cycle and shows its mapping into typical software life cycles. It is not intended to define or imply a software life cycle of its own.

IEEE/ANSI Standard 1209-1992
IEEE Recommended Practice for the Evaluation and Selection of CASE Tools
This recommended practice provides individuals and organizations with a process for the evaluation and selection of computer-aided software engineering (CASE) tools. The recommended practice addresses the evaluation and selection of tools

supporting software engineering processes including project management processes, development processes, and integral processes.

IEEE/ANSI Standard 1219-1992
IEEE Standard for Software Maintenance
This standard defines the process for performing the maintenance of software. It prescribes requirements for process, control, and management of the planning, execution, and documentation of the software maintenance activities.

IEEE/ANSI Standard 1298-1992
IEEE Software Quality Management System, Part 1: Requirements
This is Australian Standard AS 3563.1-1991. This standard establishes requirements for a software developer's quality management system. It identifies each of the elements of a quality management system to be designed, developed, and maintained by the developer with the objective of ensuring that the software will meet the requirements of a contract, purchase order, or other agreement.

SPICE products

Introductory Guide (IG). This describes how the SPICE products fit together and provides guidance and requirements for their selection and use in building sector-specific standards.

Process Assessment Guide (PAG). This defines how to conduct an assessment using the Baseline Practices Guide (BPG) and the Assessment Instrument (AI).

Baseline Practices Guide (BPG). This defines, at a high level, the practices that are essential to good software engineering.

Assessment Instrument (AI). This guides the creation and use of forms for collecting data about the processes undergoing assessment to help confirm the presence of the baseline practices.

Process Improvement Guide (PIG). This provides guidance on how to use the PAG, BPG, and AI for software process improvement.

Process Capability Determination Guide (PCDG). This provides guidance on how to use the PAG, BPG, and AI for supplier evaluation and/or certification.

Assessor Training and Qualification Guide (ATQG). This provides guidance on how to develop training programs for assessors using the SPICE standard.

(*Note:* At the time of writing, a number of these SPICE products were still at draft, review, and trial use stage.)

Appendix B
Verification checklists

The following checklists are included in this appendix:

- Requirements verification checklist
- Functional design verification checklist
- Internal design verification checklist
- Generic code verification checklist (1)
- Generic code verification checklist (2)
- Code verification checklist for "C"
- Code verification checklist for "COBOL"
- Generic documents verification checklist.

Requirements verification checklist

The checklist below is adapted from the Boeing Computer Services Requirements Checklist, as published in *Handbook of Walkthroughs, Inspections, and Technical Reviews*, 3rd edn, pp. 294–5. Copyright © 1990, 1982 by D.P. Freedman and G.M. Weinberg. Used by permission of Dorset House Publishing. All rights reserved. Grateful acknowledgment is also due to Boeing Computer Services Company.

(1) *Complete.* All items needed to specify the solution to the problem have been included.
(2) *Correct.* Each item is free from error.
(3) *Precise, unambiguous, and clear.* Each item is exact and not vague; there is a single interpretation; the meaning of each item is understood; the specification is easy to read.
(4) *Consistent.* No item conflicts with another item in the specification.
(5) *Relevant.* Each item is pertinent to the problem and its solution.
(6) *Testable.* During program development and acceptance testing, it will be possible to determine whether the item has been satisfied.
(7) *Traceable.* Each item can be traced to its origin in the problem environment.
(8) *Feasible.* Each item can be implemented with the available techniques, tools, resources, and personnel, and within the specified cost and schedule constraints.

(9) *Free of unwarranted design detail.* The requirements specifications are a statement of the requirements that must be satisfied by the problem solution, and they are not obscured by proposed solutions to the problem.

(10) *Manageable.* The requirements are expressed in such a way that each item can be changed without excessive impact on other items.

Changes to the completed requirements specifications can be controlled; each proposed change can be traced to an existing requirement; and the impact of the proposed change can be assessed.

Functional design verification checklist

The checklist below is adapted from pp. 303–8 of *Handbook of Walkthroughs, Inspections, and Technical Reviews*, 3rd edn. Copyright © 1990, 1982 by D.P. Freedman and G.M. Weinberg. Used by permission of Dorset House Publishing. All rights reserved.

Some methods of transforming specifications to reveal ambiguities, errors, and/or misunderstandings

(1) Vary the stress pattern in a sentence to reveal possible alternative meanings.

(2) When a term is defined explicitly somewhere, try substituting that definition in place of the term.

(3) When a structure is described in words, try to sketch a picture of the structure being described.

(4) When a structure is described by a picture, try to redraw the picture in a form that emphasizes different aspects.

(5) When there is an equation, try expressing the meaning of the equation in words.

(6) When a calculation is specified or implied in words, try expressing it in an equation.

(7) When a calculation is specified, work at least two examples by hand and give them as examples in the specification.

(8) Look for statements that in any way imply CERTAINTY and then ask for proof. Words such as ALWAYS, EVERY, ALL, NONE, and NEVER are useful clues to indicate unproved certainty.

(9) When you are searching behind certainty statements, PUSH THE SEARCH BACK as many levels as are needed to achieve the kind of certainty a computer will need.

(10) Be on the lookout for words that are supposed to be PERSUASIVE, such as CERTAINLY, THEREFORE, CLEARLY, OBVIOUSLY, or AS ANY FOOL CAN PLAINLY SEE.

(11) Watch for VAGUE words, such as SOME, SOMETIMES, OFTEN, USUALLY, ORDINARILY, CUSTOMARILY, MOST, or MOSTLY.

(12) When lists are given, but not completed, make sure that there is a complete understanding of the nature of the subsequent items. Watch out for ETC., AND SO FORTH, AND SO ON, or SUCH AS.

(13) In attempting to clarify lists, as in (12), we sometimes state a rule. Be sure that the rule doesn't contain unstated assumptions.

(14) Look for lists WITHOUT EXAMPLES or examples that are TOO FEW or TOO SIMILAR to each other to explicate the rule.
(15) Beware of vague verbs such as HANDLED, PROCESSED, REJECTED, SKIPPED, or ELIMINATED.
(16) PASSIVE VOICE constructions are also traps. Since the passive voice doesn't name an actor, it's easy to overlook who is doing the work.
(17) Be especially on the lookout for COMPARATIVES WITHOUT REFERENTS.
(18) PRONOUNS are often clear to the writer and not to the reader.

Internal design verification checklist

The checklist below is adapted from pp. 313–15 of *Handbook of Walkthroughs, Inspections, and Technical Reviews*, 3rd edn. Copyright © 1990, 1982 by D.P. Freedman and G.M. Weinberg. Used by permission of Dorset House Publishing. All rights reserved. Grateful acknowledgment is also due to Boeing Computer Services Company.

The checklist presumes that internal design is described in at least two levels of abstraction with a separate document for each: a preliminary design and a subsequent detailed design.

The Boeing Computer Services preliminary design document review checklist
(1) Are the preliminary design objectives clearly stated?
(2) Does the preliminary design document contain a description of the procedure that was used to do preliminary design or is there a reference to such a procedure? Such a procedure should include the following:
    (a) A description of the design technique used.
    (b) An explanation of the design representation.
    (c) A description of the test procedures, test cases, test results, and test analyses that were used.
    (d) A description of the evaluation procedures and criteria that were used.
(3) Is there a list of the functions that are to be provided by the computing system?
(4) Is there a model of the user interface to the computing system? Such a module should provide the following:
    (a) A description of the languages available to the user.
    (b) Enough detail to allow you to simulate the use of the computing system at your desk.
    (c) Information about the flexibility/adaptability/extendibility of the user interface.
    (d) Information about tutorials, assistance, etc., for the user.
    (e) A description of the functions available to the user and the actual access to those functions.
    (f) An appreciation of the ease of use of the computing system.
    (g) The detail required to formulate and practice the user procedures that will be required to use the computing system.
(5) Are there models and/or descriptions of all other interfaces to the computing system?
(6) Is there a high-level functional model of the proposed computing system? Such a model should be accompanied by the following:
    (a) An operational description.
    (b) An explanation of the test procedure, test cases, test results, and test analysis used to ensure that the model is correct.

(c) An evaluation of the model with respect to the requirements to ensure that the requirements are satisfied. (Preliminary design does not provide detailed results that allow for detailed qualitative and quantitative analysis.)

(d) A discussion of the alternatives that were considered and the reasons for the rejection of each alternative.

(7) Are the major implementation alternatives and their evaluations represented in the document? For each of these alternatives, you should expect to find the following:

(a) A complete, precise, and unambiguous model that identifies the modules, the input and output sets of the modules, the operational sequences of the modules, and the criteria for the execution of each operational sequence in the model.

(b) An evaluation of the model that ensures that the requirements will be satisfied. Some of the things to look for in this evaluation are:
- performance
- storage requirements
- quality of results
- ease of use
- maintainability
- adaptability
- generality
- technical excellence
- simplicity
- flexibility
- readability
- portability
- modularity.

An examination of these models should include both the functional model and the associated data models.

(c) Estimates of the costs, time, and other resources that will be required to implement the alternative. These estimates should be accompanied by the following:
- a description of the estimating technique used;
- the source of the data used in making the estimates;
- the confidence factor associated with each estimate.

(d) An identification of the modules that will be implemented as hardware and those that will be implemented as software. (Some will be a combination of hardware and software.) This should also include recommendations to buy, buy and modify, or build each module. Each recommendation should be accompanied with supporting information.

(8) Is there a recommendation from the preliminary design team to implement one of the alternatives?

(9) Is the recommendation of the preliminary design team adequately supported?

(10) Does the information presented in the preliminary design document and during the preliminary design review give you the confidence that the computing system can be implemented to satisfy the requirements to such an extent that you would use the proposed system?

Generic code verification checklist (1)

Data reference errors

(A)   Array, string, records, variant records, constant, and variable referencing.

   (1)   For all array references, is each subscript value an integer within the defined bounds of its dimension?

   (2)   When indexing into a string, are the limits of the string exceeded? Are there any "off by one" errors in indexing operations or subscript references to arrays?

   (3)   Is an unseen or uninitialized variable referenced?

   (4)   Is a literal used where a constant would actually work better (e.g., boundary checks)?

(B)   Storage attributes

   (1)   Does a storage area have an alias name? Is it always given the correct attributes?

   (2)   Does a variable's value have a type or attribute other than that expected by the compiler/interpreter?

   (3)   If a pointer or reference variable is used, does the referenced storage have the attributes expected by the compiler/interpreter?

   (4)   If a data structure is referenced in multiple procedures or subroutines, is the structure defined identically in each procedure?

(C)   Storage allocation

   (1)   Is storage allocated for referenced pointers?

   (2)   Are there explicit or implicit addressing problems if, on the machine being used, the units of storage allocation are smaller than the units of storage addressing?

(D)   Other

Data declaration errors

(A)   Variable and constant attributes

   (1)   If a variable is initialized in a declaration, is it properly initialized and consistent with its storage type?

   (2)   Are variables assigned the correct length, type, and storage class?

(B)   Variable and constant usage

   (1)   Are there any variables with similar names? This is not necessarily an error, but it is a sign that the names may have been confused somewhere within the program.

   (2)   Have all variables been explicitly declared within their block? If not, is it understood that the variable is shared with the enclosing block?

(C)   Other

Computation errors

(A)   Data type discrepancies

   (1)   Are there any computations using variables having inconsistent data types?

   (2)   Are there any mixed-mode computations?

   (3)   Are there any computations using variables having the same data type but different lengths?

(4) Is the target variable of an assignment smaller than the right-hand expression?

(B) Arithmetic, relational, Boolean, and pointer evaluation errors

(1) Is overflow or underflow in an intermediate result of a numeric computation possible?

(2) Is it possible for a divisor/modulus to be zero?

(3) If the underlying machine represents variables in base-2, are there consequences from the resulting inaccuracy?

(4) Are there any invalid uses of integer arithmetic, particularly divisions?

(C) Design evaluation errors

(1) Where applicable, can the value of a variable go outside its meaningful range? For example, a variable PROBABILITY might be checked to ensure it is in the closed interval [0,1.0].

(2) For expressions containing more than one operator, are the assumptions about the order of evaluation and precedence of operators correct?

(D) Other

Comparison errors

(A) Arithmetic

(1) Are there comparisons between fractional or floating point values represented in base-2 by the underlying machine?

(2) Does the way in which your compiler/interpreter evaluates Boolean expressions affect the program?

(B) Boolean

(1) Are assumptions about the order of evaluation for expression with more than one Boolean operator correct?

(2) Does each Boolean expression state what it should state? Are the operands of a Boolean operator Boolean?

(C) Conversion

(1) Are conversion rules for comparisons between data or variables of inconsistent type or length handled?

(D) Comparison operators

(1) Are they correct?

(E) Other

Control flow errors

(A) Entrance/exit conditions

(1) If the language contains a statement group concept, are the ENDs explicit and do they match their appropriate groups?

(2) Will the program, module, subroutine, or loop eventually terminate if it should?

(3) Is there a possibility of premature loop exit?

(4) Is it possible, owing to the conditions upon entry, for a loop to never execute? Does this represent an oversight?

(5) If the program contains a multiway branch, can the index variable ever exceed the number of branch possibilities?

(B) Iteration

(1) What are the consequences of "loop fallthrough" (e.g., while condition never false)?

(2) Are there any "off by one" errors?
(C) Non-exhaustive decisions
  (1) Are there any? (For example, if an input parameter's expected values are 1 or 2, does the logic assume it must be 2 if it is not 1? Is the assumption valid?)
(D) Other

Interface errors

(A) Parameters and arguments
  (1) Do the number and attributes (e.g., type and size) of parameters received by a module match those sent by each of the calling modules according to design-level documents? Is the order correct? This applies to user-defined and built-in functions and libraries too.
  (2) If a module has multiple entry points, is a parameter ever referenced that is not associated with the current point of entry?
  (3) Are constants ever passed as argument? If the receiving subroutine assigns a value to a constant parameter, the value of the constant may be altered.
(B) Evaluation
  (1) Does a subroutine alter a parameter that is intended to be only an input value?
  (2) Do the units of each parameter match the units of each corresponding argument? (Example, degrees vs. radians?)
  (3) If global variables are present, do they have similar definitions and attributes in all referencing modules?
(C) Other

Input/output errors

(A) Files
  (1) If files are explicitly declared, are their attributes correct?
  (2) Have all files been opened before use?
(B) Errors
  (1) Are EOF or I/O error conditions detected and handled?
  (2) Are there grammatical errors in program output text?
(C) Format errors
  (1) Does the format specification agree with the information in the I/O statement?
(D) Storage area
  (1) Do the I/O area storage size and record size match?

Portability

(A) Storage classes/sizes
  (1) How is the data organized (i.e., packed structures)?
  (2) Is a character set assumed (i.e., collating sequence)?
  (3) Is there an assumed set of system parameters (HP-UX system return codes)?
  (4) Has the type of code to be generated (e.g., different object code generated) been considered?
(B) Other

Other checks
(A) Listings
    (1) If a cross-reference listing is produced, search it for variables that are never or singly referenced.
    (2) If an attribute listing is produced, use it to ensure that no unexpected default attributes have been assigned.
(B) Warnings
    (1) If the program compiled successfully, but produced "warning" or "informational" messages, check each. These indicate you may be doing something of questionable validity.
(C) Robustness
    (1) Is the program or module sufficiently robust? That is, does it check its input for validity?
    (2) Is there a function missing from the program?
    (3) Are there memory errors (e.g., heap and/or stack)?
(D) Other

Generic code verification checklist (2)

The checklist below is adapted from pp. 337–8 of *Handbook of Walkthroughs, Inspections, and Technical Reviews*, 3rd edn. Copyright © 1990, 1982 by D.P. Freedman and G.M. Weinberg. Used by permission of Dorset House Publishing. All rights reserved.

General questions to keep in mind when reviewing code

Function
(1) Is there a concept, an underlying idea, that can be expressed easily in plain language? Is it expressed in plain language in the implemented code?
(2) Does the function of this part have a clear place in the overall function of the whole, and is this function clearly expressed?
(3) Is the routine properly sheltered, so that it may perform its function reliably in spite of possible misuse?

Form
(1) Whatever style is adopted, is it clean and clear when taken as a whole?
(2) Is it meaningful to all classes of readers who will see it?
(3) Are there repeated code segments, whether within or between routines?
(4) Are comments useful, or are they simply alibis for poor coding?
(5) Is the level of detail consistent?
(6) Are standard practices used?
(7) Is initialization properly done, and does the routine clean up after itself?

Economy
(1) Are there redundant operations for which there is no compensating benefit?
(2) Is storage use consistent, both internally and with external specifications?
(3) How much will it cost to modify? (Consider the three most likely future modifications.)
(4) Is it simple?

Code verification checklist for "C"

This is an inspection checklist by development for development. Most of the items have to do with maintainability and readability, not reliability. Also, most of the items could be enforced by a custom compiler or a syntax-checking utility. Developers should not repeatedly invest in expensive inspections that could be automated.

Functionality
(1) Does each unit have a single function?
(2) Is there code which should be in a separate function?
(3) Is the code consistent with performance requirements?
(4) Does the code match the detailed design? (The problem may be in either the code or the design.)

Data usage
(A) Data and variables
    (1) Are all variable names in lower case?
    (2) Are names of all internals distinct in 8 characters?
    (3) Are names of all externals distinct in 6 characters?
    (4) Do all initializers use "="?
    (5) Are declarations grouped into externals and internals?
    (6) Do all but the most obvious declarations have comments?
    (7) Is each name used for only a single function (except single-character variables)?
(B) Constants
    (1) Are all constant names in upper case?
    (2) Are constants defined via "# define"?
    (3) Are constants that are used in multiple files defined in an INCLUDE header file?
(C) Pointers typing
    (1) Are pointers declared and used as pointers (not as integers)?
    (2) Are pointers not typecast (except assignment of NULL)?

Control
(1) Are "else_if" and "switch" used clearly? (generally "else_if" is clearer, but "switch" may be used for non-mutually-exclusive cases and may also be faster).
(2) Are "goto" and "labels" used only when absolutely necessary, and always with well-commented code?
(3) Is "while" rather than "do-while" used wherever possible?

Linkage
(1) Are "INCLUDE" files used according to project standards?
(2) Are nested "INCLUDE" files avoided?
(3) Is all data local in scope (internal static or external static) unless global linkage is specifically necessary and commented?
(4) Are the names of all macros in upper case?

Computation

(A) Lexical rules for operators
  (1) Are unary operators adjacent to their operands?
  (2) Do primary operators "->" "." "()" have a space around them? (should have none)
  (3) Do assignment and conditional operators always have a space around them?
  (4) Are commas and semicolons followed by a space?
  (5) Are keywords followed by a blank?
  (6) Is the use of "(" following function name adjacent to the identifier?
  (7) Are spaces used to show precedence? If precedence is at all complicated, are parentheses used (especially with bitwise ops)?

(B) Evaluation order
  (1) Are parentheses used properly for precedence?
  (2) Does the code depend on evaluation order, except in the following cases?
    (a) expr1, expr2
    (b) expr1 ? expr2 : exp2
    (c) expr1 && expr2
    (d) expr1 || expr2
  (3) Are shifts used properly?
  (4) Does the code depend on order of effects (e.g., i = i++;)

Maintenance

(1) Are non-standard usages isolated in subroutines and well documented?
(2) Does each unit have one exit point?
(3) Is the unit easy to change?
(4) Is the unit independent of specific devices where possible?
(5) Is the system standard defined types header used if possible (otherwise use project standard header, by "include")?
(6) Is the use of "int" avoided (use standard defined type instead)?

Clarity

(A) Comments
  (1) Is the unit header informative and complete?
  (2) Are there sufficient comments to understand the code?
  (3) Are the comments in the units informative?
  (4) Are comment lines used to group logically related statements?
  (5) Are the functions of arrays and variables described?
  (6) Are changes made to a unit after its release noted in the development history section of the header?

(B) Layout
  (1) Is the layout of the code such that the logic is apparent?
  (2) Are loops indented and visually separated from the surrounding code?

(C) Lexical control structures
  (1) Is a standard, project-wide (or at least consistent) lexical control structure pattern used?

e.g.,

```
{
}
```

or

```
while (expr) {
stmts;
}
```

etc.

Code verification checklist for COBOL

The checklist below is adapted from the IBM COBOL Program Checklist, as published in *Handbook of Walkthroughs, Inspections, and Technical Reviews*, 3rd edn, pp. 339–44. Copyright © 1990, 1982 by D.P. Freedman and G.M. Weinberg. Used by permission of Dorset House Publishing. All rights reserved. Grateful acknowledgment is also due to International Business Machines Corporation.

Identification division
(1) Does the prose in the REMARKS paragraph function as a complete prologue for the program?

Environment division
(1) Does each SELECT sentence explicitly define the external (system-dependent) specifications for the file?

Data division – file section
(1) Are the file definitions (FDs) in the same order as their respective SELECT sentences in the environment division?
(2) Do the record and data item names conform to their usage?
(3) Does each FD contain comments regarding:
    (a) File usage (recording mode, block size, record length, embedded keys, etc.)?
    (b) Amount of activity (updated how often, used every time program is run, etc.)?
    (c) Interaction with other data items. (Do its records contain objects of OCCURS...DEPENDING ON clauses? Is the length of its records dependent on such an object elsewhere in the program, etc.?)
(4) Is the file sorted or merged?
(5) Are statistics kept on file activity in a given run or series of runs?
(6) Is the correct balance struck between specifying complete file attributes in the program and specifying some of them dynamically (such as block size, maximum record length); that is, if a file is designed to be flexible in the given program, is it defined as flexibly as needed?

Data division – working storage and linkage sections
(1) Do the data item names conform to their usage?
(2) Does each data item (except for elementary items of obvious usage – subscripts, etc.) contain comments regarding:
    (a) Characteristics (fixed- or variable-length, maximum allowable length, etc.)?

(b)   Interaction with other data items? (Does this data item contain or depend on objects of OCCURS…DEPENDING ON, etc.?)

(c)   Area of use in program? (Is it used only in a certain section, or during a range of paragraphs, etc.?)

(3)   Are all data items with any kind of unifying quality placed together according to a particular scheme?

(a)   Usage (arithmetic work areas, work areas for file records, etc.)?

(b)   Commonality of purpose (everything used to process a particular file, etc.)?

(c)   Attributes (message texts, constants, etc.)?

(4)   Are all working storage items that are used as constants designated as such?

(5)   Are data items that are required to be in a particular order sequenced correctly?

(6)   Is the use of REDEFINE/RENAME in a data description justified and documented in terms of a simplification of data references, rather than reliance on the normal hierarchy of level numbers?

Procedure division

(1)   Are block comments included for major functional areas (for example, paragraph, section, segment)?

(2)   Is the module commented on in sufficient detail?

(3)   Are comments accurate and meaningful?

(4)   Does the code essentially correspond to the outline of the module documented in the remarks paragraph?

(5)   Does each paragraph, section, or segment have a homogeneous purpose which justifies and/or necessitates placing all the code together under such a grouping?

(6)   Does each performed paragraph or section document the function it accomplishes and the part of the overall logic it represents?

(7)   In a segmented program, is it clear why segmentation is necessary?

(8)   Does each segment stand alone, or is there heavy dependence on other segments?

Format

(1)   Are IFTHENELSE and DO groups aligned properly?

(2)   Are nested IFs indented properly?

(3)   Are comments accurate and meaningful?

(4)   Are meaningful labels used?

(5)   Are the clauses of complex verbs (for example, SORT/MERGE and OPEN/CLOSE) indented properly and clearly under the verb?

(6)   Does all use of GO TO conform to installation standards?

External linkages

(1)   Are initial entry and final exit correct?

(2)   Is each entry point defined correctly?

(3)   Is each parameter referenced in an ENTRY statement a 77 or 01 item in the linkage section?

(4)   Is the usage of STOP, RUN/GOBACK/EXIT PROGRAM verbs correct?

(5)   For each external call to another module:

(a)   Are all required parameters passed to each called module?

(b)   Are the parameter values passed set correctly?

(c)   Upon final exit from this module, are all files closed?

Logic
(1) Has all design been implemented?
(2) Does the code do what the design specified?
(3) Is the design correct and complete?
(4) Are the proper number of characters within a field tested or set?
(5) Is each loop executed and the correct number of times?

Program language usage
(1) Is the optimal verb or set of verbs used?
(2) Is the installation-defined restricted subset of COBOL used throughout the module?
(3) Is attention given to normal "housekeeping" requirements in COBOL (for example, setting the length of a variable-length target field before a MOVE to that field is executed)?

Storage usage
(1) Is each field initialized properly before its first use?
(2) Is the correct field specified?
(3) If a storage area is set and used recursively, is its housekeeping performed properly?
(4) Is the field initialized statically (that is, by means of the VALUE clause on its definition), when it should be dynamically (by assignment), or vice-versa?
(5) Is the use of the REDEFINES clause in the data item's definition compatible with all uses of the date item in the code?
(6) If the CORRESPONDING option of the MOVE and arithmetic verbs is used, is it absolutely clear from the data definitions which target fields will be affected (and, equally important, which will not)?

Test and branch
(1) Is the correct condition tested (IF X=ON vs IF X=OFF)?
(2) Is the correct variable used for the test (IF X=ON vs IF Y=ON)?
(3) Is each condition name, used as a test of a data item, defined as an 88-level under that data item?
(4) Is each branch target of a simple GO TO or GO TO...DEPENDING ON statement, correct and exercised at least once?
(5) Is the most frequently exercised test leg of an IF statement the THEN clause?

Performance
(1) Is logic coded optimally (that is, in the fewest and most efficient statements)?
(2) Has subscripting been used where indexing logic would be more effective and appropriate, or vice-versa?
(3) Have ERROR DECLARATIVEs been coded for files likely to have recoverable I/O errors?
(4) Are normal error/exception routines provided for:
    (a) ON SIZE ERROR – for arithmetic statement?
    (b) INVALID KEY – for start/read/write/rewrite statements?
    (c) AT END – for search/release/sequential READ?
    (d) ON OVERFLOW – for STRING/UNSTRING?

Maintainability
(1) Are listing controls utilized to enhance readability (for example, EJECT, SKIPx)?
(2) Are paragraph and SECTION names consistent with the logical significance of the code?
(3) Is each PERFORMed paragraph terminated with an EXIT paragraph?
(4) Is the use of the ALTER statement completely justified, as opposed to some sort of switch/conditional branch flow of control?
(5) Are null ELSEs included as appropriate?

Copy facility usage
(1) Is every data item definition and processing paragraph, standardized for the installation, generated in the module via the COPY facility?
(2) Is there a sound reason why the REPLACE option of the COPY statement is utilized to change any of the names of data items in the COPY'd code?

Generic documents verification checklist

The list below can be used for reviewing user manuals or any other documentation. It was adapted from pp. 356–9 of *Handbook of Walkthroughs, Inspections, and Technical Reviews*, 3rd edn. Copyright © 1990, 1982 by D.P. Freedman and G.M. Weinberg. Used by permission of Dorset House Publishing. All rights reserved.

A shopping list of faults to look for in reviewing documentation
(1) Have all phases of the document's life cycle been considered?
    (a) Is there provision for user feedback?
    (b) Is there provision for making changes?
    (c) Will changes in the system cause difficult or expensive changes in the documentation?
    (d) Is there adequate provision for distribution of the documents?
    (e) Is there adequate provision for distribution of changes to the documents?
    (f) Can documents be reproduced easily?
    (g) Can copying be prevented or controlled?
    (h) Are there available people to supplement documents?
    (i) Do the user and creators agree on the purpose of the documents?
    (j) Is there adequate provision for keeping support people current and informed?
    (k) Are tools available (e.g., fiche readers, terminals) for reading/accessing/storing these materials?
    (l) Have the documents been properly approved?
    (m) Do these documents show where they fall in the total plan?
    (n) Do the documents indicate other documents that may be used as follow-up?
(2) Are the contents of the documents adequate?
    (a) Coverage of topics
        (i) All essential topics complete?
        (ii) Have irrelevant topics been kept out?
        (iii) Topics complete, but is there completeness in detail, assumptions, facts, unknowns?
        (iv) Is technical level appropriate to level of document?
        (v) Who is the intended reader (readers)?

    (b) Correctness
        (i)   No errors of fact?
        (ii) Are there no contradictions?
    (c) Evidence
        (i)   Is the evidence adequate to support the presentation?
        (ii) Is the evidence realistic?
        (iii) Is there a clear statement of goals of the documents? Are the goals consistent?
        (iv) Does the presentation sound authoritative?

(3)   Are the materials in the documents clear?
    (a) Are examples clear?
        (i)   Used where necessary?
        (ii) Relevant where used?
        (iii) Contribute to understanding?
        (iv) Misleading?
        (v) Wrong?
        (vi) Less effective than their potential?
    (b) Are diagrams, pictures, or other visual materials clear?
        (i)   Used where necessary?
        (ii) Relevant where used?
        (iii) Contribute to understanding?
        (iv) Clearly rendered?
        (v) Misleading?
        (vi) Wrong?
        (vi) Less effective than their potential?
        (vii) Appropriate amount of information?
    (c) Is terminology clear?
        (i)   Consistent throughout all documents?
        (ii) Conforms to standards?
        (iii) Is there a glossary, if appropriate?
        (iv) Are definitions correct?
        (v) Are definitions clear?
        (vi) Is the glossary complete?
        (vii) Is there too much technical terminology?
    (d) Is writing style clear?
        (i)   Do paragraphs express only connected ideas and no more?
        (ii) Are larger logical units broken by subheadings?
        (iii) Is the fog index too high for the audience?
        (iv) Does it talk down to the typical reader?
        (v) Does it put you to sleep?
        (vi) Is there an abstract?

(4)   Are the documents adequately supplied with referencing aids?
    (a) Is there a table of contents, if appropriate?
    (b) Is the table of contents well placed?
    (c) Is there an index, if appropriate?
    (d) Is the index well placed?
    (e) Is the table of contents correct?
    (f) Is the index correct?

(i) Are page references accurate?

(ii) Are there entries for the kinds of things the various classes of users will be seeking?

(iii) Are the entries under the right titles?

(iv) Are there alternate titles for entries that might be accessed using different terminology?

(v) Are major and minor entries for the same terms distinguished?

(vi) Are terms broken down adequately, or are there too many page references under single terms, indicating that more subcategories are needed?

(vii) Are there superfluous entries?

(g) Is there a bibliography of prerequisite publications?

(i) If there are no prerequisites, is this stated?

(ii) Is the bibliography where it will be found before attempting to read the document?

(iii) Are the references complete enough to locate the publications?

(iv) Are there annotations to help the reader choose the appropriate document?

(h) Is there a bibliography of related publications which may contain further information?

(i) If this is a unique source of information, is this stated?

(ii) Are the references complete enough to locate the publications?

(iii) Are there annotations to help the reader choose the appropriate document?

(i) Does the organization of the documents themselves contribute to the ease of finding information?

(i) Is page numbering sensible?

(ii) Is page numbering complete?

Appendix C

Verification exercises

Requirements verification exercise

The following document is a requirements specification for a reservation system. Try reviewing it as if you were preparing for an inspection meeting, using the guidelines on inspections and reviews in Chapter 7 in the section on verifying requirements.

Remember that successful verification takes time. Good inspectors can take up to one hour per page of text and it's been proven to be cost effective.

Look for any ambiguities, omissions, non-testable items. Use the requirements verification checklist in Appendix B. Add to the checklist any new items you think should be checked in future documents on the basis of this particular verification.

Record the time you take to do the exercise.

Estimate the time/cost consequences if the errors you find had been allowed to migrate to later stages of development, or even to the user.

A "solution" to this verification exercise follows.

The Queen Lili'uokalani Campsite reservation system, requirements specification

The Queen Lili'uokalani Children's Center in Kona, Hawaii, has set aside family camping sites at Papawai Beach for the benefit and enjoyment of children with Hawaiian ancestry.

Objective
Develop a campsite reservation system for use on an IBM-compatible personal computer.

Reservation policy
(1)   There are three (3) different sites, with the following capacities:
    (i)   Main Camp   50 campers maximum
    (ii) Middle Road Camp 30 campers maximum
    (iii) Point Camp   30 campers maximum
(2)   There are designated camping areas at each site:
    (i)   5 areas at Main Camp
    (ii) 3 areas at Middle Road Camp

(iii) 3 areas at Point Camp

(3) Any area may be closed to the public when needed for special Agency events.

(4) Maximum of 10 people per reservation.

(5) Reservations are made no more than one month in advance. A one-month waiting period must intervene between reservations, beginning on the day the key is returned.

(6) A reservation consists of specific counts and names of adults and children. At least 30% must be children, of whom one-half must be registered with Queen Lili'uokalani as Hawaiian or part-Hawaiian children.

(7) Reservations are limited to:

　(i)　7 consecutive days while school is in session;

　(ii)　4 days/3 nights during school breaks and holidays.

(8) Reservations may be cancelled by calling at least two (2) days in advance. A "no-show" results in a warning. The second warning results in a three-month suspension of beach privileges. The third warning results in a six-month suspension.

(9) A key deposit of $10 is required. The deposit is refunded when the key is returned. Keys must be picked up on a working day and no earlier than one week before the reservation. Keys are due on the first working day following your stay. Late key return results in forfeit of deposit. Lost keys result in a three-month suspension and forfeit of deposit.

Software requirements

(1) User type: A single-user system. One user type, namely a reservation administrator.

(2) Functional environment and interface: An easy-to-use, menu-driven system that would take a computer novice less than four hours to master without the use of any accompanying documentation.The reservation system must operate in and conform to the Microsoft Windows environment.

　The user must be able to:

　(a)　log on/off the application;

　(b)　add/modify/delete names of children with Hawaiian ancestry;

　(c)　perform a backup/restore of all application data;

　(d)　make reservations/cancellations for campsites. Reservations need not be in the names of the children with Hawaiian ancestry;

　(e)　enter warning/suspension notices;

　(f)　delete historical reservations that are more than a user-specified number of months old;

　(g)　print/display reports of current warnings and suspensions in effect;

　(h)　print/display reports of future reservations by date, by name in which a reservation is made, by site, and by area;

　(i)　record key deposits and returns.

(3) Publications: User documentation is not required. Context-sensitive HELP is required.

(4) Compatibility: Must run on DOS 6.0 and Windows 3.1.

(5) Security: The personal computer may not be dedicated to this reservation system. Therefore, the reservation system and its underlying database should be protected from unauthorized access.

(6)   Installability/configurability: Software must be user installable and support a user-selectable printer configuration, without any accompanying documentation.
      Must support the following printers:
      (i)   HP LaserJet 4M
      (ii) IBM 4019 Laser Printer
      (iii) Epson LQ Series
(7)   Performance: All user operations except those whose performance is data-dependent (like query/search/report) must complete within three seconds, assuming that the computer system is dedicated to the single task of this application.
(8)   Reliability/recoverability
(9)   Serviceability
(10) Testability

Requirements specification exercise – solution

The following annotations on the text were the result of the consolidated efforts of 10 testing practitioners doing a review of the material for a period of approximately 30 minutes.

The Queen Lili'uokalani Children's Center in Kona, Hawaii, has set aside family camping sites at Papawai Beach for the benefit and enjoyment of children with Hawaiian ancestry.

Objective
Develop a campsite reservation system for use on an IBM-compatible personal computer.

Reservation policy
(1)   There are three (3) different sites, with the following capacities:
      (i)   Main Camp   50 campers maximum
      (ii) Middle Road Camp   30 campers maximum
      (iii) Point Camp   30 campers maximum

Is this a head count? A tent count? Or what?
What is the rate for each camp? Same rate or different rate?

(2)   There are designated camping areas at each site: **(no ties?)**
      (i)   5 areas at Main Camp
      (ii) 3 areas at Middle Road Camp
      (iii) 3 areas at Point Camp

What is the distribution policy? Fill an area then go onto the next one, or distribute evenly? How many campers can you put in each area? Are the areas all the same size? Co-ed?

(3)   Any area may be closed to the public when needed for special Agency events.

How to notify people who have reserved already?
What happens to people who have reserved already?
Can you move people to another area?
With what priorities?

Calendar, notifications, refunds?

(4)   Maximum of 10 people per reservation.   **(no ties to 2)?**

Do they have a minimum number required for reservation?
Is this really per site?

(5)   Reservations are made no more than one month in advance. A one-month waiting period must intervene between reservations, beginning on the day the key
is returned.

Does this mean two months?
Is this restriction by camper, or by reserver?

(6)   A reservation consists of specific counts and names of adults and children. At
least 30% must be children, of whom one-half must be registered with Queen
Lili'uokalani as Hawaiian or part-Hawaiian children.

Do only the children have to be of Hawaiian descent?
How is Hawaiian descent defined?
Live here for 2 years, born in Hawaii?
Must they be related?
Do you verify?
Where/how/database?

(7)   Reservations are limited to:
        (i)   7 consecutive days while school is in session;
        (ii)   4 days/3 nights during school breaks and holidays.

Are these fixed universal dates?
Which school schedule do you follow?

(8)   Reservations may be cancelled by calling at least two (2) days in advance. A
"no-show" results in a warning. The second warning results in a three-month
suspension of beach privileges. The third warning results in a six-month
suspension.

First warning does not get any penalty!
Does "beach privileges" mean they can reserve camp space?
No acceptance criteria for cancellation?

(9)   A key deposit of $10 is required. The deposit is refunded when the key is
returned. Keys must be picked up on a working day and no earlier than one
week before the reservation. Keys are due on the first working day following
your stay. Late key return results in forfeit of deposit. Lost keys result in a three-
month suspension and forfeit of deposit.

What if you cancel?
For one reservation?

Software requirements
(1)   User type: A single-user system. One user type, namely a reservation
administrator.
(2)   Functional environment and interface: An easy-to-use, menu-driven system

that would take a computer novice less than 4 hours to master without the use of any accompanying documentation.

The reservation system must operate in and conform to the Microsoft Windows environment.

The user must be able to:

(a) log on/off to the application; **What does this mean?**

(b) add/modify/delete names of children with Hawaiian ancestry;
    How specified?

(c) perform a backup/restore of all application data; **What kind of device does the software support?**

(d) make reservations/cancellations for campsites. Reservations need not be in the names of the children with Hawaiian ancestry;

(e) enter warning/suspension notices; **By name? what if next time reservation is made in another name? notice consists of what?**

(f) delete historical reservations that are more than a user-specified number of months old; **Should the user be notified?**

(g) print/display reports of current warnings and suspensions in effect;
    Are these by named individuals?

(h) print/display reports of future reservations by date, by name in which a reservation is made, by site, and by area;

(i) record key deposits and returns. **What about pending ones?**

What happens when the camp areas are full?
What about agency events. Are they displayed?

(3) Publications: User documentation is not required. Context-sensitive HELP is required.

(4) Compatibility: Must run on DOS 6.0 and Windows 3.1.

What kind of platform?
What's the minimum memory to this application?

(5) Security: The personal computer may not be dedicated to this reservation system. Therefore, the reservation system and its underlying database should be protected from unauthorized access.

Define. Who's unauthorized?
What other applications? (So we may simulate the actual environment)
Non-verifiable or just not accessible.

(6) Installability/configurability: Software must be user installable and support a user-selectable printer configuration, without any accompanying documentation.
    Must support the following printers:
    (i)   HP LaserJet 4M
    (ii) IBM 4019 Laser Printer
    (iii) Epson LQ Series

How much space does it take?

(7) Performance: All user operations except those whose performance is data-dependent (like query/search/report) must complete within three seconds,

assuming that the computer system is dedicated to the single task of this application.

(8) Reliability/recoverability:

Defined how? Metrics?
What happens when the disk is full?

(9) Serviceability

Defined how? Metrics?

(10) Testability

Defined how? Metrics?

More questions/issues/problems with the requirements specification

(1) May a reservation be made for a group consisting exclusively of children (with no adults)?

(2) Must the program support a waiting list for each camp site/area?

(3) Does a seven-day reservation mean seven nights or six nights?

(4) Who is penalized (issued a warning) for a no-show? Everyone in the reservation, just the adults, just the children, or just the individual who made the reservation?

(5) Regarding the waiting period between reservations, with whose name(s) is the waiting period attached? Everyone in the previous reservation, just the adults, just the children, or just the individual who made the previous reservation?

(6) What happens with four or more warnings?

(7) Is it the responsibility of the user or the application to determine whether school is in session and limit the reservation to four days?

(8) Are special Agency events handled with the same rules as other reservations (i.e., reservation can be made no earlier than one month in advance)?

(9) For any given camping area, is the reservation strictly in terms of calendar dates, with hours implied (e.g., noon until noon), or is the reservation pegged to specific hours of the day (e.g., 3 pm Wednesday until 10 am Sunday)?

(10) What are the designations (names) of the areas at each site? How, exactly, are they identified?

(11) What are the minimum memory and disk requirements of the program?

Exercise on functional design verification

The following document is a functional design for a sales commission system. Try reviewing it as if you were preparing for an inspection meeting, using the guidelines on inspections and reviews in Chapter 7 in the section on verifying functional design.

Look for any ambiguities, omissions, non-testable items. Use the checklist in Appendix

B. Add to the checklist any new items you think should be checked in future documents on the basis of this particular verification.

> *Record the time you take to do the exercise.*

> *Estimate the time/cost consequences if the errors you find had been allowed to migrate to later stages of development, or even to the user.*

> *A "solution" to this verification exercise follows.*

This exercise presumes a basic understanding of windows, pull-down menus, and item selection via mouse, as presented by most Macintosh and PC-Windows applications.

Functional design specification for ABCSALES

Preliminary version: company ABC

Company ABC sells six basic products:

(P1) pager X (purchased for $80 or leased for $5/month)
(P2) pager Y (purchased for $120 or leased for $10/month)
(P3) local paging service ($12/month/unit; unlimited usage)
(P4) cellular phone G (purchased for $500 or leased for $35/month)
(P5) cellular phone H (purchased for $270 or leased for $20/month)
(P6) local cellular phone service ($60/month/unit; unlimited usage).

> Customers must use ABC service for leased units but not for purchased units. ABC service is not restricted to customers who purchase or lease ABC equipment.

> ABC has two categories of sales personnel:

- Sales Representative (SR): sells all products
- Sales Manager (SM): sells all products and manages SRs

ABC sales commission plan

Sales representative (SR)

Each month, an SR has a base salary of $2,200, an equipment quota of 20 cellular phones plus 10 pagers and a service quota of 20 new units (any combination of pagers and cellular phones). Both purchased and leased units qualify in satisfying the equipment quota.

> For each purchased unit of equipment quota, the SR receives a 4% commission on the sale; for each purchased unit above quota, the commission is 7%. For each new lease during the month, the SR receives 13% of the monthly lease price for quota units and 18% for all units above quota; for all subsequent months in which that unit remains on lease, the SR receives 10% of the monthly lease price.

> For each new service-quota unit in a given month, the SR receives 10% of the monthly service charge. For new service units above quota, the SR receives 15% of the monthly service charge. For all subsequent months in which that unit remains in service, the SR receives 8% of the monthly service charge. An SR may receive a maximum of $700 per month in residual service commissions. An SR receives a bonus of $300 for each month in which he/she exceeds 150% of the service quota.

Sales manager (SM)

Each month, the SM has a base salary of $2,900, an equipment quota of 10 cellular phones and 5 pagers, and no service quota.

The SM's commissions on equipment (new and lease residuals) are the same as those of the SR. In addition, the SM receives 1% of all new equipment purchases and leases generated by SRs plus 1% of all SR lease residuals. The SM receives a commission of 14% for all new service contracts he/she generates. The SM receives 2% of all monthly charges for residual service contracts of SRs. The SM has no monthly cap on residual service commissions. The SM receives a $400 bonus for each month in which all SRs make their quotas.

General program functions

ABCSALES is a self-contained system which provides the following general capabilities and functions:

(1) ABCSALES has read/write access to two databases, SALES and PERS. SALES contains a complete historical record of every sales transaction (purchases as well as activations and terminations of service and lease contracts). PERS contains the names of the current SM and all current SRs. (SALES and PERS are initially empty; they are updated and maintained exclusively by ABCSALES.)

(2) For each sales transaction, ABCSALES accepts user input which defines a sales transaction in its entirety and updates the SALES database accordingly.

(3) ABCSALES allows the user to add or delete SRs and SMs in the PERS database and to transfer ownership of sales transactions in the SALES database (to ensure that all transactions have continuous ownership).

(4) On user demand, ABCSALES will generate a report (based on the SALES and PERS databases) showing the month-to-date gross income for all current SRs and the current SM for the current month, as prescribed by the sales commission plan.

Detailed functional description

ABCSALES is a single-user application which runs under the Windows environment on an IBM-compatible PC.

The execution of ABCSALES is initiated by double-clicking the ABCSALES icon in the Program Manager window. The ABCSALES window will then be displayed.

The menu bar of the ABCSALES window contains two menus: the standard Control Menu (i.e., the box in the upper left corner of the ABCSALES window) and the Command Menu. The following commands are available via the Command Menu:

- Salespers (add or delete an SM/SR, and/or transfer transaction ownership)
- Xaction (define a new sales transaction)
- Report (generate a report)
- Exit (terminate execution of ABCSALES).

Salespers

When the Salespers command is selected, a window named Salespers is displayed. The window contains the following:

(1) A list of all current SRs. Each entry in the list is a 20-character field containing the name of a current SR.

(2) A separate 20-character field containing the name of the current SM.

(3) Near the upper right-hand corner of the Salespers window is a set of five buttons that provide the following actions:

   (a) OK returns to the ABCSALES window. The SM field must contain a name.

   (b) ADD adds a new SR. When the ADD button is selected, a small window named SRadd is displayed. That window contains a 20-character field where the user names the new SR. The new SR must have a name that is unique with respect to the names of the current SM and SRs. The SRadd window contains two buttons: OK to perform the add and CANCEL to cancel it; both return the user to the Salespers window which contains the updated SR list.

   (c) XFERXACT transfers all the sales transactions (in the SALES database) owned by the selected sales person to another sales person to ensure continuous ownership. When this button is selected, the user is prompted to select the *to* sales person from the list of current SRs and SM. The user is then returned to the Salespers window.

   (d) DELETE deletes the selected sales person (SM or SR). A sales person cannot be deleted if he/she owns any sales transactions in the SALES database. The user is returned to the Salespers window, which contains the updated list of SRs and SM.

   (e) NEWSM installs the selected SR as the new SM. If an SM exists when this button is selected, then the current SM is moved to the list of current SRs. The user is returned to the Salespers window, which contains the updated list of SRs and SM.

Xaction

When the Xaction command is selected, a window named Xaction is displayed. The window contains a program-generated transaction id (an 8-digit integer, right-justified with leading zeroes) to uniquely identify the transaction, as well as the following data fields for the user to define the details of the transaction:

(1) transaction date (mm/dd/yy, with leading zero for single-digit month, day, or year)

(2) transaction id for lease/service termination (if the transaction is to terminate service or a lease, the user enters the id of the transaction which initiated that service or lease; for terminations, all other data fields on the screen, except for the date, are ignored)

(3) name of sales person

(4) product (the user must select, by clicking on it, one product from the displayed list of six)

(5) if selected product is equipment, user must select either PURCHASED or LEASED.

Near the upper right corner of the Xaction window is a set of three buttons that provide the following actions:

- ENTER to enter the transaction and return to the ABCSALES window
- CLEAR to re-initialize all data fields (to allow the user to start over with a clean Xaction window)
- CANCEL to return to the ABCSALES window with no transaction entry.

CLEAR and CANCEL ignore all data fields, but ENTER performs numerous validity checks before the transaction is entered into the SALES database. If errors are detected, the transaction is not entered into the database, and the user is informed by an appropriate message or window. The following checks are made by ENTER:

(1) The date is a valid date, and it is no later than today's date.
(2) For termination transactions, the transaction id must exist in the SALES database, and that transaction must be for a lease or service contract.
(3) The sales person field must contain the name of a current sales person (SM or SR) in the PERS database.

Report
When the Report command is selected, a report is generated and printed. The report contains the following information for each sales person:

(a) name of the sales person and title (SR or SM)
(b) monthly base salary
(c) income from equipment quota (purchases and new leases)
(d) income from equipment above quota (purchases and new leases)
(e) income from new service contracts for quota
(f) income from new service contracts above quota
(g) residual income from equipment leases
(h) residual income from service contracts
(i) for SMs, income from SRs' sales
(j) bonuses
(k) total gross income for the month.

Exit
Execution of ABCSALES is terminated by selecting either

(a) the Exit command from the ABCSALES Command Menu, or
(b) the Close command from the ABCSALES Control Menu.

Solution to exercise on reviewing functional design specification

The following annotations on the text were the result of the consolidated efforts of 10 testing practitioners doing a review of the material for a period of approximately 30 minutes.

Functional design specification for ABCSALES

Preliminary version: company ABC
Company ABC sells six basic products:

(P1)   pager X (purchased for $80 or leased for $5/month)
(P2)   pager Y (purchased for $120 or leased for $10/month)
(P3)   local paging service ($12/month/unit; unlimited usage)
(P4)   cellular phone G (purchased for $500 or leased for $35/month)
(P5)   cellular phone H (purchased for $270 or leased for $20/month)
(P6)   local cellular phone service ($60/month/unit; unlimited usage)

Customers must use ABC service for leased units but not for purchased units. ABC service is not restricted to customers who purchase or lease ABC equipment.

ABC has two categories of sales personnel:

- Sales Representative (SR):   sells all products
- Sales Manager (SM):   sells all products and manages SRs

ABC sales commission plan

Sales representative (SR)
Each month, a SR has a base salary of $2,200, an equipment quota of 20 cellular phones plus 10 pagers and a service quota of 20 new units (any combination of pagers and cellular phones). Both purchased and leased units qualify in satisfying the equipment quota.

For each purchased unit of equipment-quota, the SR receives a 4% commission on the sale; for each purchased unit above quota, the commission is 7%. For each new lease during the month, the SR receives 13% of the monthly lease price for quota units and 18% for all units above quota; for all subsequent months in which that unit remains on lease, the SR receives 10% of the monthly lease price.

For each new service-quota unit in a given month, the SR receives 10% of the monthly service charge. For new service units above quota, the SR receives 15% of the monthly service charge. For all subsequent months in which that unit remains in service, the SR receives 8% of the monthly service charge. An SR may receive a maximum of $700 per month in residual service commissions. An SR receives a bonus of $300 for each month in which he/she exceeds 150% of the service quota.

This is hard to read and keep track of. Maybe a table format would help.

Sales manager (SM)
Each month, the SM has a base salary of $2,900, an equipment quota of 10 cellular phones and 5 pagers, and no service quota.

The SM's commissions on equipment (new and lease residuals) are the same as those of the SR. In addition, the SM receives 1% of all new equipment purchases and leases generated by SRs plus 1% of all SR lease residuals. The SM receives a commission of 14% for all new service contracts he/she generates. The SM receives 2% of all monthly charges for residual service contracts of SRs. The SM has no monthly cap on residual service commissions. The SM receives a $400 bonus for each month in which all SRs make their quotas.

General program functions
ABCSALES is a self-contained system which provides the following general capabilities and functions:

(1) ABCSALES has read/write access to two databases, SALES and PERS. SALES contains a complete historical record of every sales transaction (purchases as well as activations and terminations of service and lease contracts). PERS contains the names of the current SM and all current SRs. (SALES and PERS are initially empty; they are updated and maintained exclusively by ABCSALES.)

(2) For each sales transaction, ABCSALES accepts user input which defines a sales transaction in its entirety and updates the SALES database accordingly.

(3) ABCSALES allows the user to add or delete SRs and SMs in the PERS database and to transfer ownership of sales transactions in the SALES database (to ensure that all transactions have continuous ownership).

(4) On user demand, ABCSALES will generate a report (based on the SALES and PERS databases) showing the month-to-date gross income for all current SRs and the current SM for the current month, as prescribed by the Sales Commission Plan.

Detailed functional description

How about a diagram if it's going to be this detailed.

ABCSALES is a single-user application which runs under the Windows environment on an IBM-compatible PC.

The execution of ABCSALES is initiated by double-clicking the ABCSALES icon in the Program Manager window. The ABCSALES window will then be displayed.

The menu bar of the ABCSALES window contains two menus: the standard Control Menu (i.e., the box in the upper left corner of the ABCSALES window) **(What's this for?)** and the Command Menu. The following commands are available via the Command Menu:

- Salespers (add or delete a SM/SR, and/or transfer transaction ownership)
- Xaction (define a new sales transaction)
- Report (generate a report)
- Exit (terminate execution of ABCSALES).

Salespers

When the Salespers command is selected, a window named Salespers is displayed. The window contains the following:

(1) A list of all current SRs. Each entry in the list is a 20-character field containing the name of a current SR.

How many SRs can there be? What if the user entry is more than 20 characters?

(2) A separate 20-character field containing the name of the current SM.

How many SRs can there be? What if the user entry is more than 20 characters?

(3) Near the upper right-hand corner of the Salespers window is a set of five buttons that provide the following actions:

(a) OK returns to the ABCSALES window. The SM field must contain a name.

What happens when the SM field is blank?

    (b) ADD adds a new SR. When the ADD button is selected, a small window named SRadd is displayed. That window contains a 20-character field where the user names the new SR. The new SR must have a name that is unique with respect to the names of the current SM and SRs. The SRadd window contains two buttons: OK to perform the add and CANCEL to cancel it; both return the user to the Salespers window which contains the updated SR list.

What happens when the name is not unique?

    (c) XFERXACT transfers all the sales transactions (in the SALES database) owned by the selected sales person to another sales person to ensure continuous ownership. When this button is selected, the user is prompted to select the to sales person from the list of current SRs and SM. The user is then returned to the Salespers window.

What if the "to" is the same as "from"?

    (d) DELETE deletes the selected sales person (SM or SR). A sales person cannot be deleted if he/she owns any sales transactions in the SALES database. The user is returned to the Salespers window, which contains the updated list of SRs and SM.

    (e) NEWSM installs the selected SR as the new SM. If an SM exists when this button is selected, then the current SM is moved to the list of current SRs. The user is returned to the Salespers window, which contains the updated list of SRs and SM.

No CANCEL button?
Only one SM?

Xaction
When the Xaction command is selected, a window named Xaction is displayed. The window contains a program-generated transaction id (an 8-digit integer, right-justified with leading zeroes) to uniquely identify the transaction, as well as the following data fields for the user to define the details of the transaction:

    (1) transaction date (mm/dd/yy, with leading zero for single-digit month, day, or year)

Can this be left blank?

    (2) transaction id for lease/service termination (if the transaction is to terminate service or a lease, the user enters the id of the transaction which initiated that service or lease; for terminations, all other data fields on the screen, except for the date, are ignored)

    (3) name of sales person

    (4) product (the user must select, by clicking on it, one product from the displayed list of six)

    (5) if selected product is equipment, user must select either PURCHASED or LEASED.

How is the "must" enforced?

Near the upper right corner of the Xaction window is a set of three buttons that provide the following actions:

- ENTER to enter the transaction and return to the ABCSALES window.
- CLEAR to re-initialize all data fields (to allow the user to start over with a clean Xaction window).
- CANCEL to return to the ABCSALES window with no transaction entry.

Is this the precise order that these will be in?

CLEAR and CANCEL ignore all data fields, but ENTER performs numerous validity checks before the transaction is entered into the SALES data base. If errors are detected, the transaction is not entered into the data base, and the user is informed by an appropriate message or window. The following checks are made by ENTER:

(1) The date is a valid date, and it is no later than today's date.

How is the day's date defined?

(2) For termination transactions, the transaction id must exist in the SALES database, and that transaction must be for a lease or service contract.
(3) The sales person field must contain the name of a current sales person (SM or SR) in the PERS database.

Report

When the Report command is selected, a report is generated and printed. The report contains the following information for each sales person:

(a) name of the sales person and title (SR or SM)
(b) monthly base salary
(c) income from equipment quota (purchases and new leases)
(d) income from equipment above quota (purchases and new leases)
(e) income from new service contracts for quota
(f) income from new service contracts above quota
(g) residual income from equipment leases
(h) residual income from service contracts
(i) for SMs, income from SRs' sales
(j) bonuses
(k) total gross income for the month.

Exit

Execution of ABCSALES is terminated by selecting either

(a) the Exit command from the ABCSALES Command Menu, or
(b) the Close command from the ABCSALES Control Menu.

General point and questions:

- **Error handling is ignored in the specification.**
- **What if a sales person does not meet his/her quota of sales?**
- **Throughout the specification there are verbal descriptions of algorithms – a picture or formula/table/diagram would help to amplify these greatly.**

- **There are expressions sprinkled throughout the specification which give the appearance of explaining how something is accomplished while actually failing to explain them.**
- **Examples include on page 3 "updates the sales database accordingly" – what does "accordingly" mean?**
- **Another example is "on user demand" – how is the user's demand indicated to the system?**
- **On page 4, the spec mentions a "small" window. How small is this small?**
- **The control menu is not described adequately.**
- **What about shut downs or power outages in the middle of operations? Like XFERXACT.**

More questions/issues about the specification

(1) ABCSALES appears to restrict the number of SMs to one. Also, is the Salespers window scrollable if the list of SRs is too large to fit in the window? How many SRs can report to one SM? Also, the Salespers command does not permit the appointment of a new SM from outside the ranks of current SRs.

(2) Is the equipment quota filled in the actual order in which equipment is purchased or leased? If so, is there any incentive for the sales person to push (a) pagers over phones and (b) leases over purchases?

(3) Is the commission pro-rated for a partial month in which a lease or service contract is active?

(4) What is the SM's commission on residuals for self-generated service contracts?

(5) Does the SM receive a commission on new service contracts generated by SRs?

(6) In the Xaction command for termination of a lease or service contract, no check is made to ensure that (a) the transaction to be terminated is active and (b) the sales person who is terminating the transaction owns that transaction.

(7) There is no capability to enforce the rule that a leased ABC unit must use ABC service.

(8) Nothing is mentioned about maintaining historical records (in either database) regarding changes in reporting structure (SR to SM) or sales-transaction ownership. Does ABCSALES split and pro-rate the commission for a single sales transaction to reflect a mid-month change of SM or transaction ownership?

(9) In the Salespers command:

    (a) The specification does not describe what happens if the SM field is blank when the OK button is selected.

    (b) The ADD function provides an opportunity for the user to perform or cancel the ADD. However, there is no such provision in the XFERXACT, DELETE, and NEWSM functions.

    (c) All of the functions lack definitive descriptions of the program's behavior when a user error is detected.

    (d) The precise format or syntax for the 20-character name of the sales persons is never specified.

(10) The Report command doesn't say where the report is printed, and the specific format of the report, including field widths, is missing.

(11) The Xaction command does not define any specific error messages emitted by the ENTER validity checking.

Appendix D
Validation exercises (solutions)

This is one possible solution to the exercise given in Chapter 8.

Equivalence partitioning exercise solution

External input condition	Valid equivalence classes	Invalid equivalence classes
number of course records	4	<1, >8
course name in course record	non-blank	blank
par in course record	integer	not an integer
integer par in course record	4	<3, >5
number of golfers	20	<2, >400
number of golfer records per golfer	= number of courses	not equal to the number of courses
course name in golfer record	non-blank	blank
non-blank course name in golfers' record	defined in course records	not defined in course records
golfer name in golfer record	non-blank	blank
strokes in golfer record	non-zero digit	0, non-digit
delimiter record	non-blank in column 1	blank in column 1

Boundary-value analysis exercise solution

Input conditions
(1) empty input file
(2) no course records in input file
(3) 1 course record
(4) 8 course records

(5) 9 course records
(6) blank course name in course record
(7) 1-character course name in course record
(8) 18-character course name in course record
(9) for the first (1) and last (18) holes only:
    (a) non-integer for par in course record
    (b) par=2 in course record
    (c) par=3 in course record
    (d) par=5 in course record
    (e) par=6 in course record
(10) column 1 is blank in delimiter record
(11) column 1 is non-blank in delimiter record
(12) columns 2–60 are blank in delimiter record
(13) columns 2–60 are non-blank in delimiter record
(14) no golfer records in input file
(15) 1 golfer
(16) 2 golfers
(17) 400 golfers
(18) 401 golfers
(19) course name in golfer record defined by previous course record
(20) course name in golfer record not defined by previous course record
(21) a golfer has golfer records for one less than the number of courses
(22) a golfer has golfer records equal to the number of courses
(23) a golfer has golfer records for one more than the number of courses
(24) a golfer has two or more golfer records for the same course
(25) 1-character golfer name in golfer record
(26) 18-character golfer name in golfer record
(27) for the first (1) and last (18) holes only:
    (a) number of strokes is non-digit
    (b) strokes=0
    (c) strokes=1
    (d) strokes=9

Output conditions
Note: Some output conditions are redundant with input conditions (e.g., #14, 16, 17) and do not require additional tests.

(28) all golfers receive the same total score
(29) all golfers receive different total scores
(30) a golfer receives a minimum total score (zero)
(31) a golfer receives a maximum total score (6 times 18 times number of courses)
(32) per course, all golfers receive the same score on that course
(33) per course, all golfers receive different scores on that course
(34) per course, a golfer receives a minimum score on that course (zero)
(35) per course, a golfer receives a maximum score on that course (6 times 18)
(36) some, but not all, golfers receive the same total score (checking that the rank is correct)

(37) the number of golfers is such that the report fits exactly on one page, with no room left over to accommodate another golfer (to make sure that an extraneous page is not printed)

(38) the number of golfers is one greater than the number in test (37)

(39) a golfer has a name that has the lowest possible value in the sort collating sequence

(40) a golfer has a name that has the highest possible value in the sort collating sequence

Appendix E

Bibliography

Software Testing Techniques, Boris Beizer
(Published by Van Nostrand Reinhold Company, Inc., 1983. 2nd edition, 1990, 508 pages.)
This book stresses unit level testing and covers techniques that are most applicable to the individual programmer. Boris explains:

> "no matter how elegant the methods used to test a system, how complete the documentation, how structured the architecture, the development plans, the project reviews...no matter how advanced the panoply of techniques – all will come to nothing, and the project will fail, if the unit-level software, the individual routines, have not been properly tested."

Many of the techniques presented are based on the author's first-hand experience as Director of Testing and Quality Assurance for a telecommunications software producer.

Review: Boris Beizer is a veteran of software development, and his writings reflect his depth of experience. There are more than enough advanced testing techniques in this book to satisfy the vast majority of experienced programmers, logic designers, and computer designers who need to be completely familiar with detailed unit testing technology. This book is not an introduction to software testing for software testing specialists, and is not geared toward non-programmers, nor does it pretend to be.

The Complete Guide to Software Testing, Bill Hetzel
(Published by John Wiley, 1984. 2nd edition 1988, 280 pages.)
This book explains how to test software effectively and how to manage that effort. The book covers how to define testing and how to measure it, including how to ensure its effectiveness. It does not assume the reader has specific prior knowledge, and is intended for the software practitioner or manager. It contains an overview of test methods, and an extensive bibliography.

Review: This is still a good, solid, practical, fundamental book on testing. Since the original introduction in 1984, more recent topics such as GUI testing, advances in test automation, and object-orientated testing are not sufficiently covered. But for the clear explanations for many of the software testing fundamentals that have not changed, this book is in our top three.

Managing the Software Process, Watts S. Humphrey
(Published by Addison-Wesley Publishing Company, 1989, 486 pages.)

This book provides practical guidance on improving the software development process. It explains to program managers and programmers how to determine the quality of the current process, how to make improvements to the process, and where to begin. The book is part of a series from the Software Engineering Institute at Carnegie Mellon University, and describes the techniques for assessing software organizations and the managerial topics the assessments have found most critical for improvement.

Review: We know what you're thinking. This is not a book on software testing, so why is it here? Well, testing is a process, and this landmark book details the steps of managing any software process, including testing. Besides, the book includes good material on testing and inspections. But more than that, everyone concerned with testing should be aware of the Software Engineering Institute and the five levels of process maturity that this book describes in detail.

The Art of Software Testing, Glenford J. Myers
(Published by John Wiley, 1979, 177 pages.)

Many people believe that this work by Glenford Myers was the first good book ever written on software testing. It was the first to provide practical, as opposed to theoretical, coverage on the purpose and nature of software testing. It covers testing techniques as well as psychological issues fundamental to testing. According to the preface, the book has three major audiences, namely the professional programmer, the project manager, and the student of programming. Since 1979, the professional software tester has arrived, and should be added to this list.

Review: This is a classic – the first, and the one people seem to quote. That alone makes it still worth reading despite its age. The book needs to be supplemented with one of the current ones to get both the classic and the current picture.

Other useful books related to testing

Abelow, D. (1993). "Wake up! You've Entered The Transition Zone," *Computer Language*, March.

Ackerman, A.F. (1992). "Usage Testing," *Software Testing Analysis & Review (STAR) Conference Proceedings*.

Ackerman, A.F. (1994). "Constructing and Using Operational Profiles," *Software Testing Analysis & Review (STAR) Conference Proceedings 1993*.

Beizer, B. (1984). *Software System Testing and Quality Assurance*. Van Nostrand Reinhold.

Bender, D. (1993). "Writing Testable Requirements," *Software Testing Analysis & Review (STAR) Conference Proceedings*.

Beresoff, E.H., Henderson, V.D. and Siegel, S.G. (1980). "Software Configuration Management: A Tutorial," *IEEE Tutorial: Software Configuration Management*, IEEE Cat No. EHO 169-3, 27 October, pp. 24–32.

Bogart, T.G. (1993). "Fundamentals of Software Testing," *Software Testing Analysis & Review (STAR) Conference Proceedings*.

Brooks, F.P. (1975). *The Mythical Man-Month*. Reading, MA: Addison-Wesley.

Craig, R. (1992). *Software Testing Practices Survey*, Software Quality Engineering.

Fagan, M.E. (1976). "Design and Code Inspection to Reduce Errors in Program Development," *IBM Systems Journal*, **15**(3).

Freedman, D.P. and Weinberg, G.M. (1990). *Handbook of Walkthroughs, Inspections, and Technical Reviews*. New York: Dorset House.

Gilb, T. and Graham, D. (1993). *Software Inspection*. Wokingham: Addison-Wesley.

Hetzel, W. (1973). *Program Test Methods*. Englewood Cliffs, N.J.: Prentice-Hall.

Hetzel, W. (1993). *Making Software Measurement Work*. QED Publishing Group.

Hetzel, W. and Craig, R. (1990). *Software Measures and Practices Benchmark Study*. Research Reports TR-900 and TR-903, Software Quality Engineering.

Kit, E. (1986). *Testing C Compilers*, Computer Standards Conference.

Kit, E. (1986). *State of the Art, C Compiler Testing*. Tandem Computers Technical Report.

Lewis, R.O. (1992). *Independent Verification and Validation*. John Wiley.

McConnell, S. (1993). "From Anarchy to Optimizing," *Software Development*, July.

Migdoll, M. (1993). "Improving Test Practices," *Software Testing Analysis & Review (STAR) Conference Proceedings*.

Myers, G.J. (1976). *Software Reliability, Principles and Practices*. John Wiley.

Myers, G.J., Brad A. and Rosson, Mary Beth (1992). "Survey on User Interface Programming," *CHI '92 Conference Proceedings*. ACM Conference on Human Factors in Computing Systems.

Norman, S. (1993). "Testing GUIs is a sticky business," *Software Testing, Analysis and Review (STAR) Conference Proceedings*.

Rosenbaum, S. (1993). "Alternative Methods for Usability Testing," *Software Testing Analysis & Review (STAR) Conference Proceedings*.

Tener, M. (1993). "Testing in the GUI and Client/Server World," *IBM OS/2 Developer*, Winter.

1994 IEEE Software Engineering Standards Collection, IEEE Computer Society, 1994.

Software testing tools catalogs

Testing Tools Reference Guide, Software Quality Engineering, 800 423-8378 or 904 268-8639.

Profiles hundreds of commercially available software testing tools.

Software Test Technologies Report, Software Technology Support Center, Hill Air Force Base, Tel. (1) 801 777 8057.

Summary of software testing terms, a classification of tools, and a method for evaluating and selecting software test tools.

Software TestWorld CD-ROM, Edward Kit, Software Development Technologies, Tel. (1) 408 252 8306, fax (1) 408 252 8307.

An interactive CD-ROM application incorporating the leading products and services in software testing, including tools, standards, training, consultancy, conferences and publications as well interactive demos of selected tools.

Software Management Technology Reference Guide, Software Maintenance News, Inc., Tel. (1) 415 969 5522.

Describes currently available software and services to support the management of software. Includes chapter on testing issues, tools, and resources.

The CAST Report, Dorothy Graham and Paul Herzlich, Cambridge Market Intelligence Ltd, Letts of London House, Parkgate Road, London SW11 4NQ, Tel. (44) 171 924 7117, fax (44) 171 403 6729.

Summary of tools available to support software testing, including static analysis, debugging, and test management.

Ovum Evaluates: Software Testing Tools, Ovum Ltd., Tel. (44) 171 255 2670.

Detailed evaluations of 26 leading tools for automating system and acceptance testing.

Appendix F

Sources: conferences, journals, newsletters, DOD specifications

Testing conferences

International Software Testing Analysis & Review (STAR)

STAR consists of general sessions, track presentations, a tools exposition, and pre-conference tutorials. The STAR brochure states:

> "STAR is targeted at those responsible for test and evaluation activities within an organization...It is intended to motivate and assist the working practitioner and manager in using software testing practices more productively and effectively."

A typical US conference has more than 600 attendees from all over the United States as well as other countries, including the United Kingdom, Canada, Mexico, France, Norway, Germany, and Sweden. The European Conference, EuroSTAR, is hosted by the British Computer Society's Special Interest Group in Software Testing, and is linked with the STAR conference in the USA.

Contact Software Quality Engineering
Tel. (1) 904 268 8639 (US)

International Conference & Exposition on Testing Computer Software

This conference includes pre-conference full day workshops, general sessions, track presentations, and a tools exhibit.

Contact USPDI
1734 Elton Rd., Suite 221
Silver Springs MD 20903
Tel. (1) 301 445 4400

International Software Quality Week (SQW)

SQW consists of pre-conference tutorials, plenary presentations, track presentations, tool vendor exhibits, and debates. The conference brochure states:

> "Software Quality Week focuses on advances in software test technology, quality control, risk management, software safety, and test automation."

Contact Software Research, Inc.
Tel. (1) 415 957 1441

International Conference on Software Testing
This conference is a practitioner-focused event, where testing/QC professionals share
their proven methods for improving testing and quality control throughout the systems development life cycle. Practitioners share their testing processes, test management and measurement strategies, and their most effective testing techniques. A test
tool vendor expo runs concurrently with the conference so attendees can see tools
demonstrated and have one-on-one talks with tool suppliers.

Contact Quality Assurance Institute
Tel. (1) 407 363 1111
Fax. (1) 407 363 1112

Quality Assurance Institute, Inc.
7575 Dr. Phillips Boulevard
Suite 350
Orlando, FL 32819

Journals and newsletters on testing

- *Testing Techniques Newsletter:* Software Research, Inc., 625 Third St., San
  Francisco, CA 94107-1997. (Free)
- *Software Testing, Verification and Reliability:* (ISSN 0960-0833): a quarterly journal
  published by Wiley & Sons Ltd, Baffins Lane, Chichester, West Sussex, PO19
  1UD, UK.
- *Software Quality Management Magazine:* a quarterly magazine available through
  Software Quality Engineering, 3000-2 Hartley Road, Jacksonville, FL 32257.
  Tel. (1) 904 268 8639.
- *Software Quality World* (ISSN 1042-9255): a semi-monthly newsletter published
  by ProQual, Inc., P.O. Box 337, Medfield, MA 02052-0003. Tel. (1) 508 359 7273.
- *Software Management News,* B10-Suite 237, 4546 El Camino Real, Los Altos, CA
  94022. Tel. (1) 415 969 5522.

The SEI Subscriber Program
More than 1,000 individuals from industry, government and academia subscribe to
the SEI Subscriber Program which aims to keep its members up to date about SEI
events, works in progress, and new initiatives. Publications include BRIDGE, the SEI
quarterly magazine, the SEI Technical Review – a compendium of the key technical
work SEI performed in a given year, and subscribers receive a 10% discount on all SEI
reports and a discount at their annual symposium.

Contact Customer relations: Tel. (1) 412 268 5800.

List of relevant military/DOD specifications

DOD-STD-2167A. *Defense System Software Development*, February, 1988. Includes the following individual standards:

- MIL-STD-499A (USAF). *Engineering Management*, May, 1974.
- MIL-STD-1521B (USAF). *Technical Review and Audits for Systems, Equipment, and Computer Software*, June, 1985.
- MIL-STD-480B. *Configuration Control – Engineering Changes, Deviations, and Waivers*, July, 1988.
- MIL-STD-481A. *Configuration Control – Engineering Changes, Deviations, and Waivers (Short Form)*, October, 1972.
- MIL-STD-482. *Configuration Status Accounting Data Elements and Related Features*, December, 1970.
- MIL-STD-490A. *Specification Practices*, June, 1985.
- DOD-STD-2168. *Defense System Software Quality Program*, April, 1988.

Copies of federal and military standards, specifications, and handbooks are available through:

DOD Single Stock Point
Commanding Officer
US Naval Publications and Forms Center (Attn: NPFC 1032)
5801 Tabor Avenue
Philadelphia, PA 19120
Tel. (1) 215 697 2667

Appendix G

Specific tools and tool selection

Tool selection

The following tool evaluation process describes the methods used by Software Development Technologies, a leading testing tools consultancy, in compiling Software TestWorld™, a CD-ROM based update on currently available test tools. While these methods relate to an elaborate selection process, they contain important pointers for anyone attempting proper tool acquisition.

The selection process for inclusion on Software TestWorld is based on a stringent set of requirements evolved over the previous 15 years. It is a "whole product" approach that includes evaluating each vendor's testing tools, management team, business practices, training, and technical support. An overview of the selection process is as follows:

- Review press releases and direct mail brochures that are routinely received via mail or email.
- Scan leading trade publications for ads and articles regarding new products and new releases.
- Attend major conferences and visit with tool vendors that exhibit to examine new products and new demos.
- Review detailed product literature including available vendor "white papers"; save information in a tools data base.
- Obtain software testing tools catalogs (see Appendix E) for a summary of tools available to support software testing.
- Contact the vendors, request a tool demo, run it, test it, and make notes on the product and the demo. It is surprising how many defective and generally poor quality demos exist! (Does anyone test these demos?!)

- If the product passes the above tests for quality, order a full product evaluation kit. All the major vendors worth doing business with have product evaluation programs. Some vendors provide good tutorials, some provide the product, but in general, all provide enough to make a technical evaluation of the product. At this step, SDT licenses and installs the product on its lab machines, and evaluate these processes and the actual user documentation. In addition, SDT calls the technical support hotline, whether they need help or not, to evaluate the effectiveness of the support process.
- When possible, visit the headquarters of the tool vendor. Meet with the management, examine the facilities, and discuss pricing, customer base, marketing strategy, technical support, testing references, future products, and training.
- Vendors that meet SDT requirements are then invited to begin the process of working with the company to participate on a future version of Software TestWorld.

Contact:
Software Development Technologies
Tel. (1) 408 252 8306, fax: (1) 408 252 8307

Specific tools

The lists of specific tools in this section are not exhaustive. It is a major undertaking to produce and maintain a *current* evaluation of available testing tools and their capabilities. The following should be considered best-of-breed of available tools at the date of publication.

Software testing tools summary – MS Windows approved tools

Type	MS Windows tool	Vendor
(1) Reviews & Inspections		
(i) Complexity Analysis	Panorama	International Software Automation
	Analysis of Complexity Tool	McCabe & Associates
	Design Complexity Tool	McCabe & Associates
(ii) Code Comprehension	Battlemap Analysis Tool	McCabe & Associates
	Panorama	International Software Automation
(2) Test Planning		
(i) Schedule Estimation	CodePlan	Azor Inc.
(ii) Planning Resource	Software TestWorld	Software Development Technologies
	TestDirector	Mercury Interactive Corporation
(3) Test Design & Development		
(i) Test Data Generator	TDGEN	Software Research, Inc.
(ii) Test Design	SoftTest	Bender and Associates
(4) Test Execution & Evaluation		
(i) Capture/Playback	WinRunner	Mercury Interactive Corporation
	QA Partner	Segue Software, Inc.
	Ferret	Azor Inc.
(ii) Client/Server	LoadRunner/PC	Mercury Interactive Corporation
	Automated Test Facility	Softbridge, Inc.
(iii) Coverage Analysis	Instrumentation Tool	McCabe & Associates
	Panorama	International Software Automation
(iv) Memory Testing	HeapAgent	MicroQuill
(v) Test Case Management	TestDirector	Mercury Interactive Corporation
(vi) Simulators & Performance	LoadRunner/PC	Mercury Interactive Corporation
(5) Test Support		
(i) Problem Management	Defect Control System	Software Edge
(ii) Configuration Management	PVCS	Intersolve Inc.
	CCC/Manager	Softool Corporation

(*Note*: Tools listed above in Reviews & Inspections are also useful for Test Planning.)

Software testing tools summary – UNIX approved tools

Type	UNIX tool	Vendor
(1) Reviews & Inspections		
(i) Complexity Analysis	SMARTsystem	Procase Corporation
	Hindsight	Advanced Software Automation
	QC Coverage	CenterLine Software Inc. (formerly VistaTEST from Veritas Software)
(ii) Code Comprehension	SMARTsystem	Procase Corporation
	Hindsight	Advanced Software Automation
(iii) Syntax & Semantic Analysis	SMARTsystem	Procase Corporation
(2) Test Planning		
(i) Schedule Estimation	CodePlan	Azor Inc
(ii) Planning Resource	Software TestWorld	Software Development Technologies
(3) Test Design & Development		
(i) Test Data Generator	TDGEN	Software Research, Inc.
(4) Test Execution & Evaluation		
(i) Capture/Playback	XRunner	Mercury Interactive Corporation
	Ferret	Azor Inc.
	QC Replay	CenterLine Software Inc. (formerly VistaREPLAY from Veritas Software)
(ii) Client/Server	LoadRunner	Mercury Interactive Corporation
(iii) Coverage Analysis	Hindsight	Advanced Software Automation
	Instrumentation Tool	McCabe & Associates
	QC Coverage	CenterLine Software Inc. (formerly VistaTEST from Veritas Software)
(iv) Memory Testing	Memlight	Advanced Software Automation
	Purify	Pure Software
(v) Test Case Management	TestDirector	Mercury Interactive Corporation
(vi) Simulators & Performance	LoadRunner	Mercury Interactive Corporation
(5) Test Support		
(i) Problem Management	PureDDTs	Pure Software (formerly DDTs from QualTrak Corporation)
	CaseWare/PT	Continuus Software
(ii) Configuration Management	CaseWare/CM	Continuus Software
	ClearCase	Atria Software, Inc.

(*Note:* Tools listed above in Reviews & Inspections are also useful for Test Planning.)

Appendix H
Sample lists of improvements to be implemented

This list of improvements to be implemented is a digest of individual lists compiled by delegates at the testing course on which this book is based. They came from organizations of widely varying sizes and levels of maturity.

Standardization of terminology:
- Use IEEE/ANSI definitions
- Use verification and validation
- Use testware

Product requirement specifications:
- Push for complete, testable specifications
- Set up checklists for verifying requirements
- Set up review of current requirements
- Write a specification/requirements guideline to improve test coverage

Test tools:
- Find new automated tools, including coverage
- Investigate WinRunner
- Evaluate tools
- Automate test library
- Identify code complexity tool

Documentation:
- Create boilerplate for validation test plan
- Create verification plan and verification report
- Create and use test plan outline
- Identify test deliverables (test plans)
- Document test libraries

Miscellaneous tasks:
- Begin verification of internal design specs
- Get test points in place
- Get developers to test each other's code
- Acquire understanding of and implement risk analysis for general and specific projects
- Investigate usability testing
- Investigate company support of membership in professional groups
- Investigate Software Engineering Institute

Test library:
- Organize
- Create new stress tests

This list of improvements to be implemented was developed in-house during testing training. It represents one company's experience in devising a list.

Improvements internal to software testing

Objectives:
- Improve communication
- Automate test libraries, reduce cycle time
- Find defects earlier
- Improve problem analysis
- Create repeatable test libraries, predictable results

Prioritized improvements:
(1) Automate regression testing with capture/playback tool
(2) Standards-based test documents (test plan, test procedures, etc.)
(3) Coverage analysis tool/complexity tool/white-box testing
(4) Earlier QA involvement: (subset of 2)
    (i) earlier project planning
    (ii) earlier technical planning
(5) Post-mortem overall project reviews – QA project lead 4.0.1
(6) Process test team ownership
(7) Improve QA perception
(8) Improve equipment management (resource sharing, scheduling)

Prioritized improvements external to software testing:
(1) Marketing and functional specs
(2) Better version control (i.e. lost fixes) and release control
(3) Develop unit/integration testing (find defects earlier)
(4) Timely technical reviews of project and specs

(5)   Post-mortem project reviews
(6)   Common defect data base:
    (i)   acknowledgment of found bugs
    (ii)   QA access to customer defects
(7)   Hardware reliability
(8)   Third-party project management

Index